"It's been said that great writing is an act of courage. If that's true, this is the bravest book I've ever read. Entertaining. Chilling. Provocative. Leanne Grabel creates sentences and images other writers wish they had."
—Larry Colton, author of *No Ordinary Joes* and *Counting Coup*

"Leanne Grabel breaks the rules when she writes clearly and directly about the kidnapping and rape that changed her life. Hers is the story of an artist's way, and what it means to persist in telling the truth. Grabel's voice moves between frank innocence, flights of fancy, and a devastating narrative."
—Monica Drake, author of *Clown Girl*

"The first few lines of Grabel's introduction are enough to pull you into this tempest of a book. What we've got here is a voice so new, so unflinching, wry and intimate that the story it tells is impossible to shake."
—Dan Wieden of Wieden+Kennedy

"With savvy and biting humor, this memoir recounts decades of relationships marred or ultimately doomed by the aftermath of a horrible trauma. Ultimately, Grabel finds solace and purpose in active empathy, in teaching incarcerated teenage girls how to do what she's done with the "craters and ruts" of her own wounds: to write about those wounds, dressing them "in rhinestones and clown noses, frockcoats and badass boots."
—Paulann Petersen, author of *The Voluptuary* and *Blood Silk*

"*Brontosaurus* is a scintillatingly honest book about sexual violence and how it affects a woman's life of love in profound ways over many years. Its language is visual, visceral, and funny; ironic, acrobatic, and poetic. It is also a wittily jaundiced depiction of American manners."
—Tim Barnes, author of *Definitions for a Lost Language*

"Leanne Grabel is a wonderful writer, truly unique in her outlook, brilliant and hilarious. I have always loved her work. "
—Anne Lamott, author of *Imperfect Birds* and *Faith (Eventually)*

brontosaurus

memoir of a sex life

Leanne Grabel

QUIET LION PRESS
————Portland, Oregon

Brontosaurus: Memoir of a Sex Life
©2011 Leanne Grabel

Cover and book design by Brian Christopher
Cover photo by Michael Yearout
Illustrations by Leanne Grabel
Author photo by Julie Keefe

Library of Congress Control.Number: 2011939158

Printed in the U.S.A.

ISBN 978-1-882550-47-0

First Edition

10 9 8 7 6 5 4 3 2 1

QUIET LION PRESS
7215 S.W. LaView Drive
Portland, Oregon 97219
quietlion@msn.com

contents

Author's Note:

Thanks to Dan Wieden, Brian Christopher, Michelle Alderson, Mary McGurk Conway, Tim Barnes, Larry Colton, Monica Drake, Randy Chambers, and Paulann Petersen, all early readers of this book. A special thanks, of course, to my daughters Lili and Gina, my husband Steve, and the angel Bailey.

—Leanne Grabel

The method must be purest meat
and no symbolic dressing,
actual visions + actual prisons
as seen then and now.

A naked lunch is natural to us,
we eat reality sandwiches.
But allegories are so much lettuce.
Don't hide the madness.

—Allen Ginsberg

The brontosaurus was immense. The size of five elephants. It was one of the largest dinosaurs on earth, and also one of the dumbest. That's a horrible combination.

The brontosaurus was long-necked, thick-limbed, sloppy-lipped and gluttonous. Herbivorous, the brontosaurus gobbled thickets of foliage compulsively all day long without chewing. Then it had to devour stone after stone in order to grind those thickets into digestible swatches.

The female brontosaurus was oblivious of her femalehood. Motherhood? Forget about it. She lived to eat. Knocked up, she'd drop her eggs on the ground with no guilt like so much panty lint as she plodded along on her meandering, ill-fated chomps. She had to eat landscapes in order to sustain her tremendous size. Babies? Who had time for them?

I tell you this because there is a brontosaurus in this book, gigantic and stupid. Like an elephant in a room, but five times the size. Rape. It's rape. Rape stands in the middle of this book like a brontosaurus. Rape opens the book, and then devours a large portion of the rest of the book, glutton that it is.

There are also small tales of reaction and effect, hilarity, confusion, sex, love, not-love, sadness, oddities, jokes. All of the stories have jokes.

I liked how it felt when I wrote this book, even though it felt like it was somebody else's book. A couple times I was jolted by a random jerk, a shiver, or even a short, deep sob, however. It always came out of nowhere, fast, like an asteroid. It reminded me these stories are mine.

Every time I wrote a sad part, it felt like some of my sorrow got sucked out and dribbled over a cliff. Every time I wrote an ugly part, it felt like some of the ugly got gutted, lumped up and lugged away on shabby carts with stupid wheels by buff and sturdy workers. Every time I told a joke, I laughed.

I like how it feels to know you're reading this now. I changed almost everyone's names, especially the innocent. And I changed some of the tiny, voiceless details because sometimes rhythm or lyricism won out over precision. But I never altered important details. Never. These are the essentially true stories.

brontosaurus

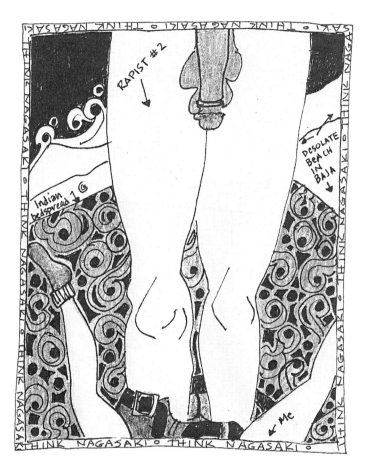

ONE

The Worst First

Dolls by the thousands
are falling out of the sky.
—Anne Sexton

Hasta Luego, Innocence

It was late March, southern tip of California. Hotter than hell with a fever. My two friends and I were heading down to Baja for spring break. None of us had ever traveled without our parents before. Not really. We were zipping about, we were envisioning, we were crackling with excitement and fear and all that.

We left Jill's mother's house in San Diego around four on a Sunday afternoon, as if it mattered. We figured we had at least another four hours of light before we had to set up camp on the Baja beaches. We were listening to King Crimson's "In the Court of the Crimson King":

I'm on the outside looking inside.
What do I see?
Much confusion, disillusion
All around me.

Exactly. But it was 1972, and the three of us, albeit naive and hesitant, were ready to party.

Jill began driving in her brother's borrowed Ford van. Within minutes, we were into the dusty decrepitude of Tijuana, with its salty, smelly itch like an old scab. We snaked along the coastline. Another car would pass every five minutes or so. It was blastingly hot. I was thirsty as hell.

"I'm dying for a Fresca," I said. "Anybody else want anything?"

"I'll take a Pepsi," Jill and Daniel answered in perfect unison. We all giggled low in our throats, easily amused. There was such a rare illumination off the waves. It turned the white of the waves to nacre, a swizzle of pearls.

"Let's stop," I said. "Wanna stop? The ocean is blowing my mind. Look at it out there? It's so beautiful! We have to stop. Pull over . . . okay?"

Jill always did what I said back then, and she pulled over to the side of the road near a long hedge of some kind of Mexican beach shrubbery. It was just like what I'd hoped for. I felt loose and alive, scared and wonderful. The beach was as beautiful and as empty as my cabinet of misfortune. The glimmering waves were the crown of my liberation at last.

Daniel pulled out the container of chicken, the coleslaw, and a few sodas from the cooler. He and Jill sat down, kicked off their shoes, and pulled out a chicken leg. I heard a rustling behind us in the shrubbery and saw the bushes trembling as if something were in them, emerging from them. What was it? There was nothing around us. No one. Who was it? Fear squeezed me like a girdle.

I looked over at Jill and Daniel. They were chomping on their chicken legs. Their own legs were straight out in front of them, and their cheeks were all smeared with red barbecue sauce. They looked like toddlers, messy and content. They were completely oblivious.

The Rapists

Two men in raggedy black ski masks ruggled out of the shrubbery like Mesozoic tongues. One of them had a rifle and the other had a sheathed thing that dangled from his pelvis. A sharp tip pointed up and out a hole in the bottom. It looked like a vicious penis, and symbolically, I guess it was.

Everything bright was sucked out of me, as you can imagine. The assumption of living was an obsolete sensation now. Mundane hunger and thirst were obsolete sensations now. I was an immediate member of a horrible, unlucky club now: The Those Who Are Probably Going to Die in an Ugly Way or At Least Think They Are Club.

I kept staring at that vicious hide thing bouncing against that one man's thigh, and that infinite black hole at the tip of that rifle and it was like staring at Death. Death was there. I couldn't believe it.

Everything changed in that moment. I aged, what, twenty years? Forty years? A hundred years? The pressure was enormous to keep breathing so I had to be smarter than I'd ever been in my life, more perfect than ever. Or else I knew I would die.

There we sat, three babies watching a gorgeous end-of-day illumination in the Mexican sea foam that looked like a swizzle of goddamned pearls. There we sat, three babies watching the sun boldly stroke its brush across the flaming sky as it lay its head down upon the horizon. There we sat facing Death.

"Can I help you?" I asked sweetly as I nudged Jill and Daniel to deeper alert. Although these guys looked like rodents from the bowels of Hell, a flicker of optimism sparkled into my head for one second like a crystal goblet on a searing surface, like Tinkerbell at Bergen-Belsen.

Maybe they are just passing through, I thought for a second. Maybe they are just going swimming. Maybe they want to hang out and talk about our respective cultures. I could tell them about that report I did in seventh grade about Goya. Wait. Goya was Spanish, not Mexican. Stupid me. Maybe they like us. Maybe they won't take out generations of rage at the American imperialistic machine on me and my friends. Maybe they won't turn us into gringo carnage. Maybe they'll think I'm Mexican. Yes, that was it, my only hope. Maybe they'll think I'm Mexican, like everyone else does, and they won't spear me, broil me, rip me, sear me, eat me like a goddamned pot of greasy white stew.

I thought that for one second.

The men were giggling and gabbing in Spanish. The air was bloated with Peril. Confusion and Shock were there, too, on our side. Excitement was probably there for them. Stun, Denial, Automatic Pilot were there. Adrenaline was there. But Fright was on the goddamned throne. I kept hearing sounds that sounded like *mort*. I kept hearing *mort* and I knew what it meant. We were dead. We were so dead.

Four flat black eyes stared out from the shadows of those ugly mask holes. Those guys looked like beetles. Their heads looked like scrotums. Their tongues stuck out those knitted holes grotesquely, like slathering, pink membranes. Their teeth looked nasty, greenish, against the seedy black.

Then they pointed those weapons with intention at my soft spots. It was a despicable and tragic moment in my life. Because in that moment, Fear took root in every cell of my body, branded me instantly, like radiation. It was, in fact, exactly like radiation. Radiation way over the acceptable limit.

I looked up and down the beach, searching for saviors. There was nothing, nobody. Not a shadow or a bump. Just sand. A hedge of shrubs. A piece of wood. We were defenseless before these creatures with their weapons. There was nobody to help us. Everything stopped breathing for an instant. The silence was so urgent, the fish began gasping, whispering to each other about the peril. There was such an ominous gurgle.

"What do you want?" I asked. "Just take what you want and leave us alone." I was demanding, begging. "Here's my purse. Take it all. I think there's $34 in there. Take it. It's yours."

"Here's my wallet," Daniel said. "Take whatever you want. Here. Take my money." His voice was shaking.

And the scrotumheads kept mumbling in Spanish, walking around the van, giggling, looking inside the van, walking around us, looking at us, giggling, mumbling to each other. They kept pointing at our heads, our bellies with those things. I kept hearing the sound mort. I couldn't believe it. We were going to die. My life now was about desperately trying not to die, waiting to die.

"You want the van?" I said pointing to the van. "Take it. Take the van. Jill, give them the keys. They can have it. Who cares? Give them the keys."

"No way," Jill said, waving her arms absurdly around as if warming up for the Series. The keys were invisible, gripped in one of her large, freckled hands.

"Give them the damn keys. Don't be stupid." I couldn't believe she was choosing now to debut a pouty insolence.

Then, with one quick swipe, the guy with the sheathed thing bouncing against his pelvis grabbed the keys from Jill's hand. He looked at the other guy and laughed. They shifted gears.

Moo

They rifle-butted us into the back of the van like livestock. And we acted like livestock, bumping into each other, grunting and mooing.

They tied our hands behind our backs with greasy ropes, blindfolded us with rags they kept pulling out of their back pockets. They bound us back-to-back, wing-to-wing, our heads stiff with fright, touching hard. Somebody ran hands over my nipples, two hands, smelled like old garlic.

My legs started shaking. The shaking started out as a regular trembling kind of shaking, as if I were cold, but soon escalated until my legs were slapping together as if audience, thigh to thigh, making loud, flapping noises. I was embarrassed, but had absolutely no control over my legs.

"Sorry," I kept mumbling to Jill and Daniel, tied up against me, bouncing as I bounced, as we traveled to our deaths.

"It's okay," they kept repeating.

"It's okay."

My body was skewered by Fright, head to toe, by this inimitable, ultimate fright. It was like electro-shock therapy. I was practically convulsing, although my mind was whip-tight.

Jill, Daniel and I said nothing at all to each other the whole time. Our captors, however, kept blabbing away.

In My Mind

I kept seeing my piano, my blond wood piano. I'd played Beethoven's "Fur Elise" probably five hundred times on that piano. I got a dollar every time from my father, who adored Beethoven.

"Rita, get my pants," he'd roar at my mother, as if it were he and I together in the game, my mother, the batboy.

He made me practice the piano every morning before the sun rose for over a decade, even on Saturdays. He screamed at me every morning, although I would have practiced on my own, was going to. I didn't like to cause trouble.

I missed everything, all the donuts, the ballgames, the time Mary got her voice back after her tonsil operation, the sleepovers. I had to practice Bach and Mozart, Liszt and Haydn.

On that beach, I kept thinking about how I was never going to have a boyfriend now. I was going to die on that beach, ripe, untasted, gored, splattered to smithereens. It made me feel so awful. So sad.

Then my jaw, the poor thing, the martyr, girded so tightly, it still hurts.

The Facts About Ultimate Fear

During moments of ultimate fear, completely and solely about survival, beyond fear, a person's heart speeds up dramatically, squeezes harder, while in the human brain, norepinephrine pumps out, focus sharpens, memory's honed, blood pressure rises, blood flow increases, oxygen and glucose bulk up. There is a shunting of blood flow away from the gut, toward the brain and the muscles of the arms and legs during fear. The spleen releases red blood cells in mass quantities, allowing for more oxygen to aerate the muscles. The liver converts glycogen to glucose, a more accessible sugar. Breathing becomes heavy on purpose so extra oxygen can get to the lungs. The pupils dilate for better vision. Opiates act on the brain to dull pain, so pain does not impair the fight for survival, so nothing impairs survival.

—J. Douglas Bremner, *Does Stress Damage the Brain*

My Body Lost Its Grip

Several of my body parts, besides just my thighs, began to act afool. I suppose they were retreating, trying to take a backseat to my brain and my muscles. My body knew instinctually that's what I needed. My brights and my brawn. That's what I needed right then, for strategic planning, operational guidance, and protection. Or survival was not assured. Repeat: Survival was not assured.

I had gas. Strange gas. I was tied up to Jill and Daniel, knees under my nose, anus flaring, and I started popping out these little whiffy ones, like fireworks in the distance, and I couldn't control it. I couldn't stop.

"Sorry, excuse me, sorry, sorry," I kept mumbling into my gag, the garlicky cloth tightly gripping my lips in a distorted position.

Was I aware of the absurdity of my politesse? I don't know. But it was also funny. I laughed when I farted. Farts are always good for a laugh.

The Ugly

Jill's brother's van, driven by a Mexican wearing a ski mask with one hand on a rifle and a buddy with a knife riding shotgun, crunched to a stop on what sounded like pebbles. I peeked out a thin crack at the side of my blindfold and saw the guy with the sheathed thing go into a small shack. There was a light bulb on a frayed cord dangling from the ceiling of the crippled porch. It seemed to be the only light for all eternity. The rifle guy kept his eyes on us, his hands on the gun in position.

About five minutes later, the guy with the sheathed thing came out with a big, brown, well-handled grocery bag. Then he drove for a few minutes, and stopped again. I peeked out but saw nothing but blackness, the black of the back of the most desolate closet in the cosmos. I couldn't even see my hand when I held it right in front of my eyes, when it was brushing my lashes.

They opened up the side of the van, untied our legs and pulled us out. They took our blindfolds off, but kept our arms and mouths tied up. One of them pointed the rifle at Daniel, then butted him away somewhere behind the van into that horrible black widow of a black Bajan night.

That's when the guy with the sheathed thing finally unsheathed the sheathed thing, pulling out a saber, its lacinating edge slathering like a ravenous cat.

"Come on, guys, let us go, guys," I could hear Daniel pleading as the guy with the rifle led him away.

"Take my wallet. Take my watch. It's all yours. Come on. Let us go, man. Don't do anything stupid."

I could hear Daniel begging for his life.

Then I swear I heard shots. I was sure I heard shots. Oh my god. Two shots. They shot Daniel. The dying had begun. My brain steamed.

The rifle guy came back and rifled Jill and me down onto

an Indian bedspread he had pulled out of the van. The saber guy took Daniel's sleeping bag and unzipped it, then whipped it out, spreading it somewhere in the utter blackness. The saber guy sat down on the blanket in between me and Jill so it was boy/girl/boy/girl.

From the wrinkled brown bag, he pulled out a bunch of rasty branches of decrepit looking marijuana. He rolled a magnificent joint the size of his arm, using an entire piece of opened-up newspaper for the paper.

My arms were now slapping around like my legs. It was indeed the dance of the damned. Terror, the hound, was barking through my body.

The saber guy pulled the whole refrigerator out of the van onto the sand. He pulled out everything in it—the coleslaw, barbecued chicken, the sodas. Then he gave all of us a soda.

"I don't drink this kind of Pepsi," I said, burrowing the can into the sand. Jill looked at me hard and slightly shook her head.

"Oh, well," I mumbled, realizing the absurdity of my worrying about calories at a time like this. I opened the Pepsi. I pretended to take a sip. I took a sip. It was probably the third time in my whole life that I had tasted regular Pepsi. My mother didn't allow me to drink it. It tasted delicious, but it was kind of sweet. Too sweet.

Then the guy with the rifle pulled out a bottle of tequila. He took a gulp and passed it to Jill. She passed it to me. I pretended to take a little sip, then just decided to take a little sip. I decided it was good politics to have whatever they were offering. It might make them in a better mood, less vicious. In fact, I couldn't believe Jill wasn't at least pretending to have some tequila. I looked at her hard.

They lit the joint that was the size of a salami and passed it around. I pretended to take some. It got all over my face. I coughed and coughed. Then I sucked some in through my mouth. Jill didn't even pretend to take the slightest toke. It pissed me off.

Headlines

I began to see headlines.

    Stanford Students on Spring Fling Slaughtered
        in Baja Tragedy.
    Valedictorian Beheaded on Baja Beach.
    An American Tragedy Out West.

Cherry Pop

The rifle guy got up and rifled Jill over to the sleeping bag area out there in the outer utter blackness, while in the inner utter blackness, I was suddenly under the point of that satanic saber.

I heard Jill shuffle away, envisioned her long, skinny legs, bony ankles, long freckled feet in cool, strappy sandals, schussing away through the sand. I noticed a new, disturbing static in my ears, like a tremendous flock of migrating birds somehow being thwarted, a low, multitudinous moaning.

The saber guy pointed me down onto the Indian bedspread, all crumpled beneath us like the dress of a dead girl. I lay down, the dead girl.

He pointed me to pull down my pants. And I did, leaving them rumpled around my ankles. (They were sailor surplus denim bells.) He pushed me down. Got on top, the ski mask right in my face. The gash of his mouth. The smell of garlic and grease in my mouth. His body on me. In me. My fear. His penis was pushing. The kissing was toothless and hard. The penis was poking and pounding.

I was frozen, of course on purpose. I made myself unable to feel. I held myself taut and closed as if pinching my nose to avoid a stink.

But truthfully, I wanted to feel it, at least for one split second. I mean, Jesus. It was sex. I'd never had sex before. Not all the way. It was this long-anticipated moment of a lifetime. My god. Loss of Virginity. The Popping of the Cherry. I had to try to feel it for a second, even if it was happening in Hell. I had to feel it for a second. I had to.

Did I? I think I did, for a fraction of a second. I felt it, without the enormous cords attached.

And then I lay there, flat, floating, plotting, envisioning the worst, swiping it away, envisioning survival. My body was like a pipe dangling from my brawny head.

My brand new Mexican blouse, with its gorgeous embroidery, was hiked up to my neck. My large breasts were smashed down by gloved hands, frightened and flaring.

"Grunt."

The head said, "Grunt."

Then it got off and the other head shuffled over. It didn't even pull up its pants. They were pooled at its feet like a puddle of piss.

I was lying flat, spread, like the last piece of bread in the loaf. It lay on me. The same smell. The same scratch. The same paws. The same pounding. I flung my body out.

Hope Smells Like Coconut

When the rape part was over, it was all about whether they were going to let us go. Or kill us. It was now or never. I hoped as hard as I could, as hard as I had ever hoped times a million, one split second after the second one got out of me and off me, that they weren't going to kill me now.

I wondered if Jill was somewhere out there, sticky, shocked. She could be dead. There was no sound except the ocean, which sounded just like the inside of my head. They were both roaring. My head's ocean, though, was amplified about a million times by Fright.

I lay there hoping with everything I had that this wasn't the part where I got shot through the eye, or gouged in the belly, or worse. Oh my God!

I envisioned everything ugly I had ever seen or heard. They might slice off my breasts! They might ax off my head. I thought of everything grisly. Oh my God. I was popping with fear.

The two men buttoned up, then rifle-butted Jill and me to get dressed and back into the van. They tied us up again, tied the blondfolds back on, but they didn't do a very good job. I could easily see out the sides.

The saber guy walked away and quickly reappeared with Daniel. I couldn't believe it. I thought for sure I'd heard shots. I thought he was dead. I was so happy for a moment. Maybe we weren't soon to become Hash of the Privileged (though Innocent).

They got back in the van and drove. We bounced around in the back like sacks of defeat. My legs were slapping together violently. I was waiting for one of them to turn around and shoot me in the eye, or the brains.

My favorite clothes from childhood started spinning across my mind. There was my daffodil-yellow, dotted Swiss nightgown. My aquamarine, dotted Swiss shift with the white lace collar I made in Home Ec. The facing under the arms sucked, it was all puckery. But the color was breathtaking. It made my skin look like butter. Even I could tell.

My raspberry wool shirtwaist went by. It was the first form-fitting dress I ever had, with its wide pink faux alligator belt. I had no real curvaceousness at twelve, but when I wore that dress, I think you could just get a whiff of my fermenting feminine juices. I could certainly feel them brewing when I wore that dress.

I saw my majorette boots prance by, their thick heels and golden tassels like the manes of Palominos. I saw those silly, little-girl high heels with their stretchy straps and their glittery heels. I saw the trampoline park and felt the rush of the spinning sky as I back-flipped for the first time, first one on the block.

I saw Ovaltine at Gina Millican's tall white house with its tall green columns. I saw her tall beautiful mother with her tall, slick hair. Everybody called her gorgeous, but I kept seeing her discontent, taut around the eyebrows, pulling her whole face into an ugly point.

Mrs. Millican was always dressing for cocktails. Her husband, Gina's father, was kind of the opposite of her. He was sweet and redheaded, freckled and cute. Kind of like her dappled lapdog. I saw my Speedo bathing suits—the gold and black striped one, the red and black striped one, the turquoise and black striped one.

I saw the surface of all those aquamarine swimming pools, splashing and rippling. I saw me racing. Taking off from the block. The 50-yard butterfly. The 50-yard breaststroke. The 200-yard Individual Medley.

I remembered my math class, senior year. Mrs. Alverson, who didn't like me. She didn't like me at all. She told my parents I was shallow. Deft, but shallow. She told them it would catch up with me someday. That comment haunted me. It still does.

Sandy Poofs of Dust

The rapists kept driving around. They were quiet. There was just the sound of tires crunching over pebbles and sand. Then they stopped in a smooth blackness. They got out of Jill's brother's van, tore out the seats as if ripping gigantic teeth from their roots with a nauseating crackle. They stripped off the paneling, tossing big sheets of it onto the beach like dried skin. They cracked off the drawers. They took the pan of chicken, the bowl of coleslaw, the cassette player, tapes. Cat Stevens. King Crimson. Emerson, Lake and Palmer. Bob Dylan. Joni Mitchell. They took them all. They took our backpacks, journals, my butterscotch suede, fringed, Wild Bill Hickock jacket. Picture sun-kissed English caramel. Fringe! Rows of it. Picture the best jacket ever. They took it. They took the foot mats. They snapped off the mirrors.

Then they untied us, took the blindfolds off, and screamed, "Go! Vamanos! Vamanos!" They tossed the keys back at Jill's feet and they screamed, "Go! Go!"

And they walked away. They didn't say another word. They just walked away, creating little clouds of sandy dust.

I kept expecting one of them to turn around, crouch, and blow me apart at the pelvis, or the ear, to stab me in the breast, or the heart. But they didn't. They just kept walking, creating tiny poofs of sandy dust. It was the happiest moment of my life.

TWO
Details

In Time

I got raped thirty-eight years ago. Weird. It was so long ago, people who weren't even born then are already dead. Richard Nixon, a horrible caricature, was President of the United States. The Vietnam War was flashing on and off the TV screen, electrifying, shocking, breaking hearts in real time, for the first time. There was animosity between decades, races, sexes, philosophies. Sometimes it seemed like there was purpose for a second. Then later it seemed like it was all just for style and fun. It went away.

Gas cost thirty-five cents per gallon in 1972. Stamps cost eight cents. Minimum wage was $1.45. Median household income was $9,012.38. Popcorn at the movies cost less than an arm and a leg. Technology was just crowning the womb of young minds. Prozac and the cell phone were brand new on the market. Pong came out. Mark Spitz was a smalltown Jewish girl's Jewish-American hero. Angela Davis, with her fabulous hairdo, was sent to jail, released from jail.

Pablo Neruda won the Nobel Prize for literature. Jim Morrison and Igor Stravinsky were found dead. John Lennon and Yoko Ono co-hosted the Mike Douglas Show for a week. "A Clockwork Orange" came out. Elvis, greasy and gaudy like the fry upon which he gorged, played Madison Square Garden, sideburns like pork chops. Eminem was born. Mia Hamm. Amanda Peet. Watergate, Laos, chaos. You've heard it a trillion times.

Sorry-Ass

In 1972, I was a naïve, funny, dour, chubby, greasy, explosive, slow-to-bloom college sophomore. I was attending Stanford University on a full State of California scholarship. It was based upon my gender, my 4.0 GPA from Amos Alonzo Stagg Senior High School, my relatively high math SAT scores, and all the offices I held, and all the clubs I was in, and all the posters I made.

The SAT scores weren't really that high, but they were impressive for a girl from a small, dusty town back in 1968. Almost nothing was expected from girls back then, especially not in math.

I was blurry about everything else besides logarithms and cosines back then. And disgruntlement. I was excellent at disgruntlement.

I had no alternative vision, no aesthetic, no balance, no emotional intelligence. I just knew I didn't like things as they were.

There were puddles at my feet, the yellow brine of my disappointment. I was slipping in the puddles, the grace of my childhood long gone. I'd grown thick. I led with my bloat, the sharp part of my mind.

But goddammit, I was truly innocent. And underneath my wry, sour, sassy façade, I was hopeful. Stupidly hopeful. I felt I'd done everything that was wanted and I was waiting for and expecting my reward. And what was that? A great boyfriend, a great job, a great house on the water.

Jill's Fault

It had been Jill's idea to head down to Baja for spring break that year. It had been Jill's idea to camp along the hot white beaches with all the other fun-loving, long-legged college students going down there that year. At least, that's what she'd heard.

Jill was the only one of us who could rise up off her angst long enough to have an actual idea about something to do other than just sit around and think about the provocative, magnificent, newly discovered circle of SUFFERING inherent in adult living.

Also, Jill had a car, a great car, a '69 spinach-green Beetle.

Jill was tall, thin, blonde, tan, smart, had a great record collection, a cute spinach-green Beetle, and several ideas. But when you looked closely at Jill, there was a strange stretch to her. Her elbows stuck out like broomsticks. Her skin, mad with freckles, had unusual creases. Her teeth were too large, her face too long. Her posture slumped as if life had already slapped her silly one too many times in a row, which it had.

And Jill spoke in a breathy, severely quiet voice. Her voice was so whispery, in fact, most people, including myself, had to ask her to repeat almost everything she said at least once if not twice. It was extremely irritating and I often lost my temper when I couldn't hear her and kept having to say, "What? What?"

Sometimes I screamed at Jill and told her it was idiotic for her to speak so quietly. She always scooped up my anger and rubbed it into the skin of her long freckled arms like lotion.

Packing for Doom

Jill started making lists of what she thought we needed for the road trip to Baja, like pillows and matches and food that could travel. I told Jill I'd bring a bowl of coleslaw. I'd use my grandmother's coleslaw recipe with the white onions and the brown sugar grated into the dressing.

Jill said she'd bring barbecued chicken, use her father's barbecued chicken recipe for the first time since he died. She told us he died one night in Thea's room, all of us lying on the bed. Then she never brought it up again, nor did anybody else.

Jill didn't cry or even tear up when she told us that first time. But we did. Thea was sobbing. I was definitely crying, but trying to hide it. Jill did tear up when she mentioned her father's barbecued chicken recipe this time, though, and so did I. I considered it a very hopeful sign for the both of us.

Daniel, the only other person who wanted to go, said he'd bring Fresca, Pepsi, cookies, and pot. Jill's brother had shown us a place to hide it, tucked away deep within the recesses of the camshaft or something.

Daniel got his hair cut short like a kiwi so he wouldn't arouse suspicion at the Mexican border. American males were being targeted, even American men like Daniel, with his sweet dimples and his white boat shoes and his tongue-depressor frame.

Daniel, the Bone

Daniel Capalino was an only child from an Italian family that immigrated to San Francisco in the first few years of the twentieth century. His grandfather was that old guy in the brown wool overcoat who bought land early and then sat in the park across from the cathedral in North Beach for decades playing bocce so slowly, his bored and over-worked wife's face aged between turns.

Gregory Corso, Herbert Huncke and other wasted Beat legends, still drinking like the truly parched, would stumble by, avoiding appointments with their cardiologists. Then they would die, while Daniel Capalino's grandfather was still sitting in the park playing bocce so slowly, his bored wife aged between turns.

Daniel Capalino was strikingly thin, very thin, way too thin, so thin I noticed how thin he was every time I saw him. He had chronic stomach-aches and was always hugging his stomach, sitting and standing concave.

Daniel's mother, only twenty miles away from our dorm, visited often. She was an annoying, round, over-wrought woman in puffy sleeves and a floral apron that never came off. She hogged all the energy in any room, leaving nothing but memories of nourishment for Daniel and his father. No wonder they were both as thin as lines. They had to flatten themselves against planes to survive her.

Yet

Daniel and his father had the most adorable dimples, like little blue lakes in the shadowed landscapes of their craggy faces.

THREE
Right After

> They were afraid of dying but
> they were even more afraid
> to show it. They found
> jokes to tell.
>
> —Tim O'Brien

Dross, Scree, Slag, Detritus

Jill, Daniel and I got back into our original positions in the van, its guts chewed up and spit out. Jill drove, sitting on the ghost of the front seat, which consisted of springs, strings, a few strips of vinyl upholstery. Daniel sat on the floor in what used to be the shotgun position, clutching his bony knees as if he were a staple, a paperclip. I sat in the back like a defeated slab of granite. The silence in that van was as strident as any sound. My head was throbbing.

"Shit," I said. I felt someone had to say something. No one said anything else.

At the California border, thirty minutes away, the big-bellied American guards were mean to us. I expected fatherly, avuncular. We got fascistic.

"Get out!" they shouted, slicing through the air with their flashlights. "Get out of the van!"

They searched us and the van, top to bottom, as if we could have hidden anything in our poor vehicle that now had no seats, no pockets, no unders, no hiddens left. Devoid of any squirt of pathos, finding nothing, they let us go.

Jill drove to her mother's house. Barely thirteen hours had passed since we had last seen her. Jill disappeared into the back of the house and then reappeared with her mother. Jill's mother's voice remained disarmingly, annoyingly soft. But I could feel her accusation like flu shots. I had the urge to slap her over and over again.

Daniel and I sat on the living room furniture without moving or talking. Occasionally, one of us sighed or blew out air. We put our heads in our hands. My head was so exhausted. I'd never thought so desperately hard for such a sustained period of time in my life.

Jill disappeared and then reappeared a few minutes later with a stack of faded plaid bed sheets and a couple of pillows in sky blue pillowcases. Her mother shuffled closely behind in her fold-up slippers. They were both wearing bathrobes. They looked like a bathrobe parade. A stupid bathrobe parade, I was thinking.

"My mom's going to take me to the doctor tomorrow morning," Jill whispered to me.

"Oh," I said in a tiny little voice that reminded me of Jill's.

"I'm really tired. I'm going to sleep," Jill said. "The couch opens up into a bed, and there are more blankets and pillows in the chest over there." When she pointed, the sleeve of her robe rode all the way up to her elbow. She had such long arms. (My sleeves were always too long.) There was such a strange stretch to her. "Or one of you can sleep in the guest room. The couch in there opens up too."

"Goodnight."

"'night."

Daniel and I stared at each other, stared at our hands, stared at the arms of our chairs. My legs went crazy. They were scared out of their wits.

"I don't think I can sleep," I said.

"Are you okay?" Daniel asked, hugging his stomach.

I shrugged my lips, nodded yes.

"Well, I'm going to the guest room," Daniel said. "I'm beat."

Daniel got up and shuffled into the back of the house.

Alone With It

There was no way I could sleep. I couldn't believe Jill and Daniel were going to sleep. I was like a disco ball, hundreds of tiny mirrors reflecting horror. I had to think, organize, arrange, do something with what just happened. What was I suppose to do with it? I wanted to just sit there and think. I wanted to sit there and try to figure out what had happened and what it meant. And what to do next, what to say, who to say it to, what to feel. I was shaking. I was tightly upholstered in residual Fear. Was I going to stop shaking? Was I going to go crazy? Was I going to get sick and die? I had to think.

So, I was still sitting in the same chair at 5:30 in the morning when Jill's mother came out in her stupid bathrobe and jabbed, "No use crying over spilt milk, Missy!" Saliva sprayed from her lips stained by fifty years of red lipstick.

She called me Missy? I stared at her cold, beady eyes. They looked like beetles. I stared at her high, lurid nostrils showing me their tiny caves whether I wanted to see them or not. Again I had an intense desire to slap the bitch silly.

"I'm not crying over spilt milk. I'm not even crying."

I wasn't even crying.

I just wanted it to be the next day so Daniel and I could call our parents and get back to the Bay Area so I could go to the Stanford Health Center and see if I was infected or impregnated or ripped or sterile or crazy or going to die.

I sat that whole night in that chair and waited for the new tainted tomorrow. It was all I could do.

New Tainted Tomorrow

"I'm not going to tell my parents what happened," Daniel said the next morning. "I'm not kidding. I'm just going to tell them we got held up and robbed."

"Maybe I shouldn't tell mine either," I said, not having even considered keeping such a magnificent secret.

"Hi, Mom," I heard Daniel say into the phone. "Ummm, well, we got held up and robbed last night," he barged right in. He was gripping the phone for dear life with one hand, hugging his stomach with the opposite arm.

"They got our wallets. Yes. They got everything."

"No. Yes. I'm okay. She's okay. She's okay. Yes. Okay."

"Yes, okay," he said. He hung up the phone. It rang immediately. It was his parents calling right back. They'd bought us tickets for San Francisco, flying out of San Diego at noon. They'd be at the airport to pick us up.

I called home next. As soon as my mother said, "Hello?" I started crying, then sobbing. I was making sounds I'd never made before.

"We got held up last night," I sobbed. "These two Mexicans tied us up and gagged us...and...took everything."

"Did they . . .? Did you . . . ? Did they . . . ?"

"Yes," I sort of burbled.

"My God," she said.

That is as explicit as it ever got between my mother and me. Neither of us have ever said the word rape to each other. We have just lead right up to it, then twitched or winked or nodded or shrugged to imply.

I understand this avoidance. It's a horrible word. There is such a piercing but slimy physicality to the word. It's so dark and membranous. It's too much to hear out loud, especially if you're the mother (even if your feelings are barricaded).

(Eggs Over Hard)

Twenty years later at Thanksgiving, three or four bloody marys under all of our belts, my sister, as she often was, blatant and in her cups, recalled that morning I called home with such strange and horrible news. My sister said my mother came back to the breakfast table and said grimly to my father, who was just about to scoop up a large bite of scrambled eggs, sautéed mushrooms and onions,

"Something horrible has happened to Leanne."

My father said nothing, sat there ripping out the innards of a round loaf of San Francisco extra sour, tossing little white bread balls onto the table, silent except for the sound of his ripping and chewing.

"She was robbed and attacked in Mexico."

I've tried to imagine what each of them could have felt that morning. I'm sure my mother went to stone. And my father, well, perhaps his heart was punched. Perhaps it was already pulverized.

I'm sure my parents blamed me, blamed Jill and Daniel, even blamed Stanford. And I'm sure my father blew a toxic gust of ire at my mother, as he always did.

Saying "Rape"

Daniel and I flew to San Francisco that afternoon. Daniel's parents picked us up at the airport and took us back to their house in Redwood City. I was starting to feel really scared about what could be wrong with me. I just wanted to go to the health center as soon as possible so I could do whatever a person was supposed to do when she got raped.

Unfortunately, this was before rape crisis centers or women's advocates, before Post Traumatic Stress Syndrome. I didn't expect there to be much of a procedure in place, but I didn't expect it to be as god-forsaken as it was out there in the rape world.

"Don't say anything to my parents about . . . you know," Daniel said. We were sitting in his den, waiting for dinner. We were once again sitting in large chairs, staring at our arms. "They won't be able to deal with it. They really won't." Daniel kept making me promise.

"I won't. I won't."

It made me feel like I was wearing a chinstrap. I felt like I was swimming underwater wearing nose plugs and a chinstrap.

And I was worrying about having to say that word rape the next day. I'd have to say it to the receptionist at the Health Center. I'd have to say it to the nurse. I'd have to say it to the doctor. I wasn't sure I could do it.

Daniel dropped me off on campus at eight the next morning. I walked up to the receptionist behind her big, long desk and whispered,

"I was just raped in Mexico."

"What?"

"I was raped."

I watched her pleat. Her forehead looked like a land of canyons. She squinted up at me.

"Have a seat."

I sank down into a lobby chair. I saw a girl I sort of knew from my Literature of the Revolution class.

"What are you doing here?" she said.

"Oh," I said, sighing deeply, "I went to Baja with some friends on Saturday, but we had some trouble. We got held up and . . . stuff . . ."

I kind of nodded, caricatured a shrug.

The receptionist directed me to follow a large nurse back into one of the examining rooms. The nurse had a phenomenally large and round ass, and her peach-colored uniform pulled tightly across it so it was hard to ignore. I watched her ass, trying to imagine what it could possibly look like in the enormous flesh.

The doctor darted in as if he were being followed, and started watching it too.

"Yes?" he asked, skinnily.

"I got raped the day before yesterday in Baja," I said as quietly as I could.

"What?"

"I got raped."

"Disrobe, please," he said, distracted, staring at that ass.

"What were you doing down there to begin with?" he asked, pulling on his latex gloves, smoothing them and shaping the curves between his thin fingers over and over.

I hated him. He was an unsympathetic sonofabitch. He brusquely attached the freezing speculum, scraped off some vaginal cultures with a long Q-tip, gave me a bottle of morning after pills, a bottle of antibiotics, and nudged me out the door. That was it. There were no lullabies, no comforting words, no suggestions or referrals.

"You know, you're lucky to be alive," he said with a hiss. I felt like crud, a worm.

Please Pass the Analgesia

Disassociation takes a variety of forms, one of which is analgesia, becoming numb, both physically and emotionally. Analgesia can be experienced as a physical or emotional numbing. The body may feel frozen or weightless.

—Dusty Miller, *Women Who Hurt Themselves*

Zombieland

I walked back to my trailer and sat on the gold tweed couch in a strange, square trance. No one was there except me. There were probably thirteen people on the whole campus, and that's how it was going to be for days. Everyone else was off skiing in Utah or Switzerland, snorkeling in Maui, or home in the bosom of Mommy and/or Daddy.

I didn't turn on the stereo or the television. I just sat there. I felt like mist, like mud, thick, ponderous, light, dark, invisible. I felt like a flat-faced figurine in the vault of the dead.

The next day, my mother and brother came to Palo Alto to have lunch with me. We went to a woodsy, Palo Alto bistro. I could tell by the slightly awkward twist of my mother's pretty lips she didn't know how to act, what to say or do. Neither did my brother. Neither did I, but I felt responsible.

We sat outside and all ordered the same thing. Chef's Salad, blue cheese dressing, coffee, and a roll. We chomped away. I was sure we were all thinking hard, trying to find the right things to say.

Finally, to ease the immense discomfort, I began to act like Richard Lewis—self-deprecating and silly. I began to make jokes about the shame, beating the ironies to death. I did this routine throughout lunch.

"You know, during the whole thing," I told my mother and my brother, "I couldn't stop farting. And every time I farted, I said, 'Excuse me, excuse me' like a parrot."

I chuckled. They stared at me, waiting for direction, while I was waiting for them to offer me the same.

"See, Mom. I never forgot my manners," I said, with no edge nor ownership.

She stared at me, lips tightly closed but cocked.

"At one point, they handed me a regular Pepsi instead of a Tab, and I wouldn't drink it because of the calories."

I didn't say the word rape once, although I did say—"You know, the [nod, blink] part was actually the best part of the whole thing because they put the weapons down. They didn't have the gun or the knife in their hands during that part. Because that was the worst part, waiting to die, expecting to die. That was the worst. So the [nod, blink, rotate right hand] part was the best part, really, in a way . . ."

I didn't make eye contact when I said this. I just said it, and then went back to my salad. We all took bites, clinking our forks, wiping our hands on our napkins. Neither my mother nor my brother said anything. We just chewed. They didn't ask me any questions.

I kept chuckling and reassuring them I was fine. My voice quivered a couple of times, but I quickly smoothed it out. My legs shivered a couple times, but I hid them under the tablecloth and pretended it was a little twitch. I guess I seemed fine. Maybe I was.

After lunch, the three of us hugged stiffly, in twos, of course. We all held our hands flat, our arms stiff. Then they drove back to Stockton.

I walked back to the trailer and sat on the couch like a strange combination of nothingness and stone. I was waiting for six days. I figured Thea would know what I was supposed to do, how I was supposed to think, what I was supposed to be feeling.

To Tell Or Not To Tell

The conflict between the will to deny horrible events and the will to proclaim them aloud is the central dialectic of psychological trauma.

—Judith Herman, *Trauma and Recovery*

To Tell Or Not To Tell, Part Two

Jill and Daniel said emphatically they did not want anyone knowing what really happened in Baja, ever. They couldn't have been clearer. Oddly, obviously, my instinctual inclination was to tell everyone everything (almost) all the time. The story poured out of me as if operated by my autonomic nervous system, bypassing conscious will, as if a secretion.

The words that told the story of Baja felt like my dependable workers, sturdy, with impressive thighs, carting off the boulders of terror on their beautiful backs, back and forth, over and over, excavating my new huge canyon of terror.

Yes, I thought the telling and retelling of the story relieved things. It was an instinctual, optimistic theory, perhaps the most optimistic of my life.

Shaking, Part Two

"I wonder when this is going to go away," I said to Phil, as we were lying on his bed in Ecology House, about to make out. My legs were flapping together like the hide wings of a bellows. It was two weeks after Baja. School had started again and everyone was back.

Phil and I had just started dating before spring break. This was our first date since, perhaps our third date ever. Just as we began to kiss, my upper body began to tremble, then to shake dramatically. It was the oddest sensation to lose control of my body like that again, there.

Phil, the son of two Connecticut psychiatrists, had these piercing lime-green eyes that were lit with judgment, ringed by thick, black lashes.

"Jesus, why are you shaking?"

I was afraid to answer. There was so much accusation and panic in his voice.

"Well . . . something really weird happened to me during spring break."

I told Phil the two-minute version. The two-minute version had become the official version. I downplayed the drama with my stupid, sad jokes. I tried to soothe the shaking.

"Weird. I was shaking like this when it happened," I said.

It was a stupid thing to say to the son of psychiatrists. It was like throwing veal to a lobo.

"My God," said Phil, jumping up off the bed, staring at my slapping legs as if they were venomous snakes. "You better get some help. You are really messed up." Phil backed away and started buttoning up his cardigan.

"I'm not kidding. You need help."

I put all of my energy into willing my legs to stop shaking. I gritted, clenched, girded. But they just kept flapping together. Phil left. I was glad. I had already decided to stop seeing Phil even before he left. In fact, Phil was at the top of the list of people who didn't act right when I told them what happened in Baja. He was the head of the people who didn't help at all—who made me feel worse. I didn't know how I wanted people to act, but it definitely wasn't like Phil.

How Thea Acted

Thea finally got back and acted empathetic, classically empathetic, brilliantly empathetic, which I think she was. Thea cried when I told her, for instance. Everyone else acted like shy trout.

"Oh, my poor Leanne," she said, throwing her arms around me. "I'm so sorry. You poor thing."

Thea hugged me tightly. But I didn't like how that felt either. It felt like bugs. Like spiders crawling on me. I shook Thea's arms off and fled to the other side of the room. I muttered with a look of apology and confusion on my face. I didn't want to hurt Thea's feelings, but I didn't want her to hug me like that either.

FOUR

Sexual Healing

> *Darling, I know you'll be there to relieve me*
> *The love you give will free me*
> *And if you don't know the things you're dealing*
> *Oh, I can tell you, darling*
> *Oh, it's sexual healing*
>
> —Marvin Gaye

Personal Therapy, Part One

There was no obvious path lined with kind feminist clinicians in Birkenstocks and Guatemalan ponchos generously cushioning my path back then. There was nobody helping. Nobody leading. There was no talk of healing, because there was no talk of wounds or harm. Nobody looked me in the eye and said they were sorry. Nobody acknowledged the awfulness. No one gave me advice. There was no procedure. I'd never known anyone who got raped. I'd never even heard of anyone.

Therapy was never mentioned. People didn't even say therapy out loud back then, except as in physical therapy. People barely said breast. I still can't say it without feeling icky.

But I was pretty sure I didn't need therapy, which I envisioned cinematically, lying on a couch before a bored, be-spectacled psychiatrist, blabbing with lots of hands. That wasn't going to happen.

I was pretty sure I was fine. All I really needed, I figured, was to have a lot of regular sex, starting as soon as possible. That way I could balance things out. It was kind of a mathematical theory. An abundance of regular sex now, the kind I'd been hearing about, thinking about, fantasizing about, and planning for years, would propel me from where I was now on the sexual graph, oh so low in the negative numbers, halfway to hell. Sex would thrust me to the right, to the good side, eventually sliding me back into the positive numbers. Sex as rape therapy. Homeopathy, really. I thought it was a good and obvious plan.

Ronny Angel

My first lover was a Palo Alto townie named Ronny. I met Ronny at a dinner party thrown by three Stanford graduate students in philosophy. They were all hobbling down cobbled paths of esoterica. One was studying Plato. One was studying phenomonology. And Tom, the third, was just sitting at this big book-strewn desk, smoking an old-fashioned wooden pipe. I have no idea what he was doing. All these guys had been at Stanford for nine years each. Nine years studying philosophical esoterica.

I was at the dinner party because I was hoping to rent a room in that house. I figured now that I'd been raped, it was absurd to live on campus.

Ronny lived next-door to these guys, while on the other side lived the football legend, Johnny Unitas. He was stewed to the max and rapidly deteriorating. (This detail, while interesting, has absolutely nothing to do with this story.) Ronny was at the dinner party that evening because he was rewiring the bathroom and happened to be there when dinner was ready. It was the early seventies, remember, and everyone was trying hard to be fair, which was not a bad thing.

Ronny was the dreamiest of them all at the table. He had the creamiest skin I'd ever seen. I sat next to him at the dinner table and couldn't help but notice the difference between the colors of our arm skins. His was the color of eggshells. Mine was pumpernickel toast. His was the color of macadamia nuts. Mine was tamari almonds. His was vanilla, mine was chocolate, and so on. You get it.

Ronny sat silent throughout the meal and I couldn't think of anything to ask him beyond, "How long have you lived next door?"

"All my life," he answered.

Ronny held his fork wrong, which embarrassed me. And he didn't go to college, which embarrassed me. But these other guys had plunged into the soundproof wonder of their own padded brains long ago. Their skin had already turned gray, the color of old books.

Ronny sat silent. I sat silent, unless one of them asked me a question related to my renting a room in their house. I did end up moving there. It was kind of awful. I developed a stress-related rash on the back of my head. I had to try to spread an ointment onto my scalp through my hair. And wear a plastic bag over it, clippied on, to bed.

Ronny had beautiful eyes, the clearest blue eyes. They were those kind of light blue eyes with an outline, night sky chasing day. I found him lovely. I loved his skin. I loved his eyes. And I loved his loopy, loose-limbed quietude. He was so different from the Stanford boys. They were all square muscle and flexed entitlement and sound.

Ronny and I had sex the day I moved into that house, two weeks after the dinner party. Ronny and I lay in his childhood bed with its tan and russet cowboy walls, ripped and curled, crayon and lassos all over them. It was late afternoon.

Ronny's skin felt so good. It felt taut and soft, warm, pliant. It was pearly, gleaming. I could barely get enough of his skin. I wanted to just lie there feeling him forever.

I only shook for a couple seconds, more like a shiver. I didn't feel scared at all. I felt embraced. I felt hugged. I felt like I was in clear, warm water. It was delicious.

But I broke up with Ronny after a month because I was embarrassed he didn't go to college. And because he was one year and seven months younger than me. And because he didn't know how to hold a fork.

Fuck Phase

After I broke up with Ronny, I had short, snap-sexual relationships with just about every male I met who had any kind of physical appeal whatsoever. The only requirements were that they go to college and know how to use a fork.

Orgasm was a cinch. I was old, old friends with the feeling. I was even good at it, I think. I could make mammalian noises with boldness and ability. It was fun to me. I could deftly play with the tonalities representative of sexual pleasure, all up and down its spectrum. I could mimic avian coos. I could mimic hyenic hysteria. I was noisy, but never loud. It was tons of fun. And it was therapeutic.

I think my record for relationship length at this time was three months. This phase went on for eight or nine years. Out of those perhaps thirty lovers, probably twenty-three broke up with me. I was the worst lover ever, frankly autistic. I wanted what I wanted, and I wanted it when I wanted it, and I didn't stop wanting it.

I hated talking, didn't talk. I hated listening, didn't listen.

I was a rape victim and I told them that.

I gained twenty pounds within the first three weeks of every relationship, trying to feed those holes. I remember this one mohair sweater I used to wear all the time back then. I always wore it when I was trying to be seductive because I thought it made me look really hot. The sweater was a beautiful shade of yellow, like lemon meringue pie. It was fuzzy and short, with bell sleeves to the elbow. It had a long, tight, ribbed waist, from right under the breast to the belly button, which peeked out. I felt so shapely in that sweater. So soft and bright. I always wore it.

Then I saw a picture of myself in that sweater twenty years later and I didn't even recognize myself. I looked like Buddy Hackett in a grapefruit suit.

Graduation

I made it through Stanford, majoring in English in the end. One of my professors told me I was a wonderful writer. That seeped in. But my writing was much too melodramatic. It took years for life to shave off the emotional pudding.

I bumped clumsily into my fancy graduation dinner at a swank Palo Alto hotel, sopping wet and dead drunk, my little sister, worse off than I, in tow. We'd been at a party in the hills around Stanford. Graduates were drinking and smoking their asses off. The strange thing was, I don't think anybody at the long Grabel table for eighteen even noticed how drunk we were.

There sat my parents, my brother, my parents' good friends, Nonie and Joe, Sylvia and Julius, Frances and Lou, Miriam and Matt. There were the McGurks. Mary, Jeanne, Adrienne, Billy. There was Nanny. I guess they were just all too excited about the Stanford part to really notice how drunk and stoned I really was. I'd never been so altered in my life.

It took all of my energy and focus to stay upright at the table, to cut the steak, to fork the steak, to put it in my mouth, to chew, swallow, to lift the water glass at the correct angle so that cubes of ice and torrents of water didn't pour down my chin. I had to accept congratulations with a shake of grace.

My sister just left the table and fell asleep on a soft chair in the corner. I would never have been able to do that in front of all those people. I could never fall asleep in the open on a chair.

FIVE
Life

> sometimes everything
> that is in you
> blazes beyond the
> concepts and the
> realities
> and you get up and . . .
>
> —Charles Bukowski

WomenSports

A couple days after graduation, with the fringe soldiers of my worst hangover ever still lingering like an effluvium, looking for their shoes, I began my life. I thought I wanted to. ASAP. Still going for the A+, I felt I had no time to waste.

Logically, I went to the Stanford Job Placement Office

and there was the listing of my dreams:

Copy Editor needed for new women's magazine.
Published by Billie Jean King. Must be college
grad. Research skills. Organizational expertise.
Multiple responsibilities. Typing.

Perfect. I had it all. Did I mention I was a competitive typist? I typed so fast, the clacking of the keys melded, became a drone, a meditation. And a Stanford degree? Are you kidding. I thought I was a shoe-in for this job. I sent in my resumé instantly, except there wasn't any internet. Instantly meant I put my resume in an envelope. Wrote a cover letter. Put a stamp on it. Walked it to the postal box.

Somebody called me the next day to set up an interview. I could smell it. Success. It smelled good, like buttery bread.

The *WomenSports* offices were in San Mateo, California, in a pale, flat, unfinished neo-modern complex off Highway 101. It was a sprout of Silicon Valley. Silicon Valley as baby.

It was also the beginning of big time women's sports, primarily because of Billie Jean King. There was such a giant buzz about her. And there was such a giant buzz in me.

I felt completely confident when I walked into that office for that interview. Except for in areas of romance and basic personal nature, I had yet to fail. I had no reason to expect to. (And Baja seemed like a burp—like a short spike of catastrophe on the velvety horizon of my future life.)

A young woman about my age in a navy-blue pantsuit and red high heels came out to greet me. She gave me a three-page article on hypdroponic farming and told me to edit it for fact, form and style. Fact, form and style. I had to say that several times to understand what it meant.

Lucky for me, I knew a bit about hydroponic farming as I had worked the summer before as a personal assistant for a sales manager at John Deere Tractors outside Tracy,

California. He was fifty-five years old with a beet red face, puffy, greased hair, white shoes, and a nonstop desire to date me. He was San Joaquin Valley to the max. Utterly.

I deleted and stetted, arrowed, dashed and syntactically colonized until I felt I had turned that article into sleek bullets of lucidity. It took fifteen minutes, which seemed too short a time to prove I was serious. So I pretended to keep working for another ten minutes exactly. Then I began to fidget obviously.

The red high heels clacked back. She took the papers, asked me to wait, and disappeared into the back. I sat there for an hour. She finally came back and told me the editor wanted to talk to me. She led me into the editor's office.

The Editor

The editor was a slender, pretty, urbane woman with bobbed chocolate-brown hair brushed to one side in a large sweeping wave that fell recklessly over only one of her beautiful green eyes. Picture chocolate-covered lime. She kept brushing the dark wave back off her brow with her creamy white hands that looked like newborn swans. Two thin, gold bracelets shone on her finely boned wrist. She wore beautiful burgundy high heels that she kept kicking off her long, thin feet. She had magnificent legs, pale as eggs. She was sexy, purposefully and successfully. I looked like a Beverly Hillbilly next to her. Maynard G. Krebs.

She asked me typical questions. I was able to answer lithely and coherently. I said, "Perfectionism is my weakness," for instance. Brilliant response I thought. What boss doesn't want to hear that? I could tell she thought I was bright and eager. And she seemed impressed with the Stanford bit. Yes, I thought it went well.

"We'll make a decision by the beginning of next week," she said, walking me out the door.

"I'm going to Stockton to visit my parents for a few days," I told her. "Would you like their number?" I felt strong.

"Yes," she said. "Someone will call either way. It should only be a few days. Thank you so much for coming in. It's been a pleasure."

She shook my hand, which looked like a fat rodent next to her swans.

As I left the editor's office, I burbled out a little air, exactly at the moment that Billie Jean King appeared. She walked right out of an office in the back and came right up to me. She said, "Hello," energetically shaking my hand so my rings rubbed together painfully, digging into my fingers. The muscles in her arms rippled like shark.

She looked like she looked. She had the shiny, near-black

hair, the aviator glasses, the clear blue eyes ringed by the darkest, curliest lashes. But she had on the ugliest clothes. Brown polyester slacks. A beige blouse with cap sleeves and snaps. It looked like gym clothes. High school gym clothes.

"Nice to meet you," I burbled.

"Nice to meet you," she blew, walking across the room and into an office labeled Lance King. Her powerful thighs audibly rubbing together.

Fame-stunned, I got into my car and drove to Stockton. I told my parents about Billie Jean King right away.

"You mean she was right there in the office?" my father shouted, incredulous, nostrils flaring, the next day at breakfast, lunch and dinner.

"Yes. It's her idea, I guess. Her money. She's funding the magazine."

"Hunh," my father snorted, impressed.

Two days later the girl in the red high heels called and offered me the job of copy editor for *WomenSports*. Yippee.

My mother, listening a half inch from my face, let out a whoop and a holler. It was the free-est sound I had ever heard her make. She sounded like a cowgirl, a seal. Then she jumped.

I didn't. I wasn't demonstrative at all. But there was joy like a little lamb nibbling sweet buttercups in the meadow of my soul.

I found an apartment in Menlo Park, seventeen miles down the freeway from *WomenSports*. It was a small L-shaped fourplex built in the twenties, lots of stucco and archways. My apartment was a minute from the freeway, and it took me only thirteen minutes on that freeway to get to my new job (off that freeway).

The fourplex was owned by an old Italian couple who seemed to be romantic and adorable, in a short-Old-World-Italian-couple kind of way. However, upon closer inspection, I determined they were a scam. The old man was as bitter as kraut, and the old lady was mean and judgmental, especially of my morality. She was always sliming me with her black eyes and long, large-nostrilled nose.

My apartment was one big white room with a couple of arched turns, and a cute, sea green bathroom with a black and white tiled floor. I had a queen-sized bed for the first time in my life. It pulled out from the wall but I detached it and placed in the middle of the floor. I covered it in a vintage brocade shawl, crimson as lips. Mary Benny had sent the shawl to my mother in high school, but my mother didn't do red. She thought red was a Mexican color.

I had a lot of sex in that red bed, although I hardly remember any of it. I do remember this one time when Eddie Van Cliburn realized he was in love with Wendy Willamette right in the middle of me. And he couldn't, he wouldn't go through with it. The sex, I mean. I was so embarrassed.

Later I realized I didn't understand what Eddie was feeling. I didn't even understand where feelings fit into it. I was focused on the pleasure. Had to feel the pleasure.

It was 1974. It was still the outer chamber of the heart of the Sexual Revolution, after all. And I'd already missed all the earlier parties in the other three chambers.

I remember a sense of bucking forward. Yes, life was moving on.

All the Cool Women from the East

The women who worked at *WomenSports* were amazing to me. I'd never met women even sort of like them. They were hip, self-contained, sophisticated women. In their late twenties and early thirties, these women had names like Rosalind and Tangerine and Gabardine. There were no Debbies, no Jills.

These women exuded sexuality and contentment, power, and what I believed was honest Gender Evolution. I was astonished and perhaps in love. Oh, I wasn't really in love with them—more with the way they presented.

They wore beautifully tailored suits with razor-sharp pleated trousers. They wore blouses like saucy whispers, unbuttoned love, nearly revealing lean cleavages. They wore magnificent boots on their magnificent legs. They wore inherited jewels.

These women were gorging on women's new strength, without bulking up. They were the tall ones at the forefront of the movement.

I was holding on by a thread. I stared too long, laughed too long and weirdly over everything they said or did, funny or not. I was clumsy around them, although inherently I'm not. I slobbered. I folded away.

My Left Stomachache

I think it was Tuesday of the second week of the job when I first noticed the dull, insistent stomachache that wouldn't go away. I kept thinking it would go away, but it kept staying, dull and insistent. The only time I could remember having any similar kind of stomachache was years before, when I was about five.

I had a vivid memory of a day throwing pebbles into a river with my grandfather. I called him Poppy. He actually played with me. And I liked to play with him because he never got mad. I never saw him mad. He was always warm and sweet. That day he was wearing a yellow knit shirt. Chocolate brown slacks. He was a dresser, Poppy was.

The rest of my family was sitting at a picnic table eating barbecued chicken, burned black, the result of my father's impatience at the grill, as always. There was also large bowl of Nanny's famous coleslaw on the table. My grandparents, Nanny and Poppy. Thank god for them. They warmed the place up.

I got a dull, insistent stomachache that day while I was throwing pebbles in the river with Poppy. It was the same as the one I had then.

When I was 5, Poppy led me over to the riverbank and lay me down on the cool bank. I was moaning and crying. He rubbed my tiny back.

"Try going eah," my father yelled. It was what my family called shitting—going eah eah, said like yeah yeah without the y's. No one knew where that came from. (Guttural Yiddish?) Poppy led me over to a clump of trees. I squatted in the dirt behind a bush and tried as hard as I could, straining the little muscles in my tiny ass, and all that came out was one tiny, dark thing about the size of a raisin, and it killed to get that out.

"Looks like a raisin," Poppy laughed, swooping me up

and laying me down on the grass, gently rubbing my back so my stomach pushed into the green coolness. And the pain finally went away.

But when I got that same stomachache that second Tuesday of my perfect, American future, there was no Poppy to soothe and fix me. And my dark, first thought was that fate was giving me the nastiest finger up the ass. Tragedy. I thought terminal cancer.

I saw him, Death, a pretty man with an oily moustache and a cheap, tight suit across his nutty crotch, zipper flap pulling.

After two weeks of stomachache, I went to a doctor. He told me he didn't think I had cancer, although he didn't really look. He said I had anxiety and I should stop drinking coffee and try to calm down. He told me to stop worrying and try to be kinder. And he told me to eat three pounds of steamed beets twice a day for two weeks.

I went home and cooked a pot of steamed beets and then hung my torso over a chair so the wooden slats pressed right into my gut. I lay into those slats. It was almost lurid, but it worked.

Within a week, the stomachache passed, along with about a boatload of bloody, freakin' beets.

The next week, in the middle of a staff meeting, our Chief Financial Officer, a large woman we called The Wizard, for her fiscal magic, her power roundness, her stacks of corporate accomplishments, her gigantic sleeves, her veil of orange hair and her meadow of freckles, said, "Don't you think Leanne has an old soul?"

She said this loudly, out of nowhere, during a short, silent lull in the middle of a discussion on Pete Hamill, I think it was. There were probably two dozen people at the meeting, and everybody heard her. The Wizard had a boom to her voice.

"An old soul, that girl," she said, staring hard at me, now

frozen, paling in my seat.

It was immediately obvious that no one else at the meeting had ever even given me a thought. Everyone seemed annoyed to have to think of me at all. No one said a thing.

Finally the editor, more impatient than ever, crossed, uncrossed, recrossed her legs. (She was wearing butterscotch suede high heels and a caramel linen sheath.)

"Shall we get back to business?" she dripped.

Later I asked Pammie what it meant to have an old soul because I didn't quite get it.

"It just means you've been around before."

"Oh," I said.

"It means you have something sad and wise in your eyes."

"Oh," I said.

Going Down at the Office

Then the editor started having an affair with the sixteen-year-old janitor. He was Billie Jean's husband's nephew, I think. He was built like a pear, such a heartbreaking shape for a man.

Then Tangerine, the beautiful art director, left her gorgeous husband, who looked exactly like Pete from "The Mod Squad," for Ginger, a blue-eyed sportswriter who had swum the English Channel. She had an equine head of prematurely white hair and a horrible stutter.

Then The Wizard started having an affair with the assistant editor, an ex-Olympic backstroker who looked like Ryan O'Neal in drag.

A few weeks later, Ginger invited me to a party at her house. All the cool women were going to be there and more. I was excited, scared. I was hoping I could fall for one of them at the party so I could be just like them. I sat in an easy chair in the living room the whole party, my legs folded under me like paperclips. I focused hard and tried to rouse sexual feelings for one of the amazing women there. I stared at the most beautiful. I waited hopefully for arousal. I tried to open up. I crossed and uncrossed my legs.

Nothing. Nothing at all. It was very disappointing.

Disillusionment

With the glorious coming of spring, my job and most of the people there began to annoy me immensely. The editor annoyed me the most. She rode around on her high white horse on one hand, and on the other hand, she was having an affair with a sixteen-year-old janitor who looked like a pear. Why would I heed her? That's what I was thinking. Plus, she had a husband and two tiny kids, forchristsakes.

Then the editor started making me edit out all the stance in the articles so as not to offend sponsors, like Clairol, our largest and most conservative.

"But I thought Billie Jean's feminist stance was the whole point of the whole magazine," I whispered to Ginger one day.

"W . . . w . . . wuh . . . wuh . . . wellll . . . well . . . " Ginger stuttered.

"What does she think about all this?" I whispered.

"Wuh . . . wuh . . . wuh . . . well..." Ginger stuttered.

My heart was thumping. These women weren't heroines at all.

Buh Bye

In a final act of job-destruction, I sent out what I thought was a very hilarious memo to the entire staff, including the editor, about how we were all in danger of being mistaken for albinos if we didn't move the whole operation outside into the sweet springtime sun.

Unfortunately, the sixteen-year-old janitor was the only one who found the memo funny. Everyone else knew it was the kiss of death. The editor became enraged and started clacking down the halls. She called an emergency meeting, and gave a big speech about how the West Coast was slack, childish, and ruled by a narcissism fed by the sun. She never once looked my way and I never once looked hers.

"I'm an award-winning East Coast magazine editor, goddammit," she boasted like a toddler. "And this is going to be an award-winning West Coast magazine run with an East Coast aesthetic, and an East Coast ethic!"

Her shell pink blouse, as soft as lamb's lips, rippled in the choppy tide of her outrage. She kicked off one gorgeous high heel, the color of lust. Her toenails were thin and arced, painted pearl.

I felt like a worm, but I didn't care. I was out. When the meeting ended, I curled into her office.

"What's the matter, Leanne?" she asked me impatiently.

"I can't be here any longer," I said. "I want to go to France. I want to go to Israel. I have a friend in a castle on the Thames. An old German boyfriend. A sick grandmother. I need to leave."

I looked down, meek and bold at the same time.

She said nothing. I sat there for too long, as usual, my skin puckering in the pool of her disdain. And then I slowly uncurled and slithered out. I felt like a happy worm.

SIX

Chaotic British Teeth

*Grisha promised himself that
one day he would be silent too.
And that he would
learn to understand words
before they were born and
after they had disappointed.*

—Elie Wiesel

My Mute & Clumsy European Vacation

I decided to do what I wanted to do to begin with and that was go to Europe like everyone else was with a thirty-pound backpack and a Eurail pass. I'd visit my Stanford friend in England, a German exchange student I slept with about four times early in my senior year, the literary haunts and impressionist museums in Paris. And then I was going to end up in an Israeli kibbutz on the Mediterranean where I would certainly find something to believe in.

Thea and her boyfriend drove me from Menlo Park, California, to Montreal International Airport in a '63 Beetle convertible, a vivid purple. It was October and as we drove through New England, I cried at the beauty of those fall trees. The minute we entered Canada, however, it began to snow. Beautiful, yes, but Thea and her boyfriend got nervous about the driving and decided to literally drop me off in front of the airport and get the hell back to Celia's parents' house in Westbury, New York, as fast as they could.

I was, at last off on my own, alone, free. I was not, however, pounding my chest with ebullience. I was not howling with hunger for life, empowered by my choices, the possibilities, the dizzy surge of adventure. Instead, I felt scared and alone, underprepared and overdressed.

I landed in London at 9:23 PM, October 20, 1974. I was so over-laden, I looked like a walking jungle-jim. Under my wool pea coat and regulation 30-pound backpack, I had on a cardigan sweater, buttoned all the way up my neck, a long underwear top, tights, wool pants, and a scarf. I don't think I'd ever been so hot in my life. I was sweating bullets.

Six steps into the terminal, and one of the straps on my backpack broke, spilling all thirty pounds of my European essentials all over the place. Now I was sweating torpedoes. The English were scurrying about me with their chaotic teeth and sensible shoes. Nobody came over to help.

I tore off the scarf first, then the coat, tore off the sweater. I tied the backpack back together, gathered up my scattered things, and, smelling like wet dog, I slunk into the British night. It was raining, though warm out. I had no hotel reservation.

At the suggestion of the driver of the tall red bus, I found a small bed and breakfast in the theatre district. I'd never heard of a bed and breakfast before, but loved the concept. It sounded so cozy and so concise.

Once inside the small room, I shook off the backpack, the underwear, the tights, the lace-up boots. I sat on the edge of the bed, naked, full-splay. And I stared at the view of these old London buildings out my window, which was also sweating. I felt so exceedingly alone and small. I felt like I was on a confusing planet of strangers. It didn't feel that good.

I tossed and turned most the night, finally got up, dressed, repacked and went to breakfast in the gray basement dining room filled with what seemed to be The Unlucky, all with wet coughs.

There were sausages, corn flakes, orange juice and buns with jellied cherries and raisins embedded on top. I found out I could also get oatmeal, but only if I asked. It struck me as so odd that morning that one of my choices was between cornflakes, sausage or orange juice. I just couldn't imagine how those three things ended up in the same category. Orange juice, corn flakes and sausage. Kind of like Andy Warhol, moths, and diapers. Wasabi, Big Hunks and your mother.

A Fabulous British Magnificence

where bosoms as smooth as white china were
nuzzled by lords dressed in houndstooth as
hungry and pale.

After one lonely night and day of odd choices, I headed for Debby, one of my trailer roommates. She was but a forty-five-minute train ride away. Stanford had satellite campuses all over the world, and Stanford in England, where Debby was, was at the Cliveden Estate. It was about thirty-five miles outside of London.

In the early sixties, fancy English lords and representatives, prime ministers and secretaries of war were caught having sexcapades with beautiful call girls who looked like Natalie Wood at the Cliveden Estate.

[Maybe you remember this scandal. It was dubbed the Profumo Scandal after John Profumo, then Britain's Secretary of War, who must have been the most lascivious. It was later made into a movie called "Scandal" starring John Hurt and Ian McKellan and Joanne Whaley, Val Kilmer's ex, but I didn't see it.]

As the train chugged slowly through London toward Cookham, I finally relaxed enough to see how beautiful London was, its old, crotchety buildings like watchworks, their curves and corners festooned with centuries of black dust.

And in the country, it was pure Disney. Little bluebirds with great senses of humor, in long skirts and aprons, flew up to my window and told me silly jokes, then braided and put ribbons in my hair.

I got off the train and walked down a lane through several perfect gardens to get to the main house.

There were six gorgeous gardens and
nary an iris repeated itself. In the
courtyard of roses the roses had tones.
You could swim in them. Dance to them.

Stanford students lounged about the grounds of this magnificent mansion with its multi-levels of arches and overhangs in sets of nine. Stanford students were reading books as fountains misted and blossomed and sparkled. Stanford students sipped tea and nibbled English biscuits, pinky fingers erect.

Stanford students were draped over ornate chairs and ottomans in sitting rooms so opulent, the sconces felt underdressed. Drapery stood dark and tall in the background, heavy with secrets.

And Debby introduced me to the most beautiful boy named Billy Friendly. He'd been hiding for a moment, softly barricaded within the luxurious fabric.

As It Turned Out

JOURNAL ENTRY:
October 28, 1974

Billy had the bluest eyes.
A blue that eyes never get to be.
His wavy black hair had a sheen.
It reflected the crimsons and rusts
of the aged British luxury.
(Billy's poor penis?)
(The size of a seed.)

I am not a person who talks about penises. In my whole life, I've probably said the word penis five, well, maybe six times, if that. But I have to tell you a couple things about Billy Friendly, and one of them has to do with his penis.

First, I want you to know that I really liked Billy Friendly. Instantly. And he really liked me. We took a long walk that first day through the English Disneyland, and we kissed and hugged and talked and kissed and talked and hugged. It was hot and elegant and delightful.

Then the next night, Billy Friendly and I took LSD together and wandered along the Thames. Suddenly the fireworks of Guy Fawkes Day rained down upon us. Having no idea what Guy Fawkes Day was, I thought the explosions signaled nuclear war, the end of the world. I clung to Billy Friendly. Luckily, that panic passed quickly. It felt okay to die with him.

Billy Friendly and I made love (sort of) the next morning, after wandering the gardens and the endless hallways of the mansion all night. We ended up in his room, in the bowels of the mansion, down long white halls with big white pipes.

As it turned out, Billy Friendly had the smallest penis I have ever seen in my life. It was smaller than I had ever imagined a penis could be. It was more like a little flesh button, a checker.

Billy Friendly's penis couldn't really go into another person, like me, for instance. Even hard and alert, it was only a nickel mint. It felt frustrating. It did. What a curse, I thought.

Billy Friendly didn't say anything about his penis at all. He didn't even get a sad or embarrassed look on his face. But I did. I still get one. Even now.

Paris

JOURNAL ENTRY:
December 1, 1974

Parisians wear tight pants.
Have tight asses.
I order a cafe au lait.
I don't try to use a French accent.
The waiter looks at me.
Curls his lip.
His curled lip.

I left the next day for Paris. Not because of Billy's penis. I just wanted to go to Paris, the landscape of my idols, the surly and experimental writers. I took a ferry and a train, in the middle of the night. It was cold and misty on the boat. Dramatic. I felt like Ingrid Bergmann.

I wanted to sit where Gertrude Stein chatted up Pablo, suggesting he keep his day job after he showed her his poetry that one time over absinthe, heavy rocks. I wanted to sit where Henri and Claude argued over the glory of lapis. Where Ernest and F. Scott started stewing their brains, grew mortally depressed.

Sans Grace

I had the fat arm of a sodden Texan draped over my shoulder like overstuffed baggage when I walked on Parisian soil for the first time. He had attached to me on the deck of the boat in the middle of the night and wouldn't detach.

He was dressed in a sequined cowboy suit, I kid you not. It was made out of several American flags. He wore red snakeskin cowboy boots and a fringed vest. I wasn't brave enough to just flat out tell him to leave me alone, although I kept looking at him with disgust. I hoped my obvious disdain would be enough to send him trotting, but it wasn't. He was daft. He yodeled and mooed when we debarked. Mooed.

Merde. This was not how I envisioned making my entrée à Paris.

Mustard

After seven years of French, I couldn't understand a word of what anyone was saying in France, except the Texan. And when I realized how linguistically crippled I was, I became too embarrassed to try French at all. I spent the entire time in Paris mute. I suppose this was actually kind of French stylistically, now that I think about it.

At an outdoor market across the street from my hotel room, I bought purple grapes, a loaf of gorgeous bread, a pound of soft, yellow cheese, and a tube of mustard. I completed the whole transaction by nod and gesture, without uttering a word. Then I sat on a bench and fell in love with Paris and mustard, something I thought I detested. I especially liked the malleable metal tube.

I strolled through Paris for five days. I saw the famous Shakespeare and Company bookstore, the Closerie des Lilas, supposedly Hemingway's favorite Montparnasse cafe. I strolled by Gertrude Stein and Alice B. Toklas' apartment on Rude de Fleurus. I saw the long, rich bars with the giant chandeliers, the rich wood booths.

The Parisian men wore well-tailored suits, a little too tight. The women wore their bodies like gowns.

And I saw art. I stood before the classic paintings of Monet and Van Gogh, and I wept at the beauty and especially the brushstrokes. I could see their brushstrokes. It was overwhelming.

On my last day in Paris, I nodded my way through the purchase of a perfect little navy wool motorcycle jacket from a street vendor along the Seine. It had a creamy satin label that said Made in Paris. I also bought a pair of thin, maroon suspenders.

I still wear both, although the coat smells its age.

The German

I left Paris to visit Strusil, the German medical student I had met and slept with three times at Stanford the previous summer. He had been a foreign exchange student living in the house of one of my friends.

Strusil was living outside of Freiburg in a tiny one-room farmhouse in the Black Forest. He was taking classes at the University of Freiburg.

Strusil was attractive, golden, powerfully built. But there wasn't even a wisp of a flicker of a spark between us. Still, I came to visit him on another continent.

I panicked a little when the French train personnel were replaced with the Germans at the French/German border. Who could ignore the devastating history of the place? All I could envision when I heard that frightful, gutteral language were the stiff arms, the black boots, the square napes, the caterpillar moustaches, the trains. What Jew could escape the fear of a German train?

When I got to the Freiburg train station, it was midnight and there was a thick mist, like ghosts of the barbaric past. Strusil wasn't even there. Instead, a bouncy couple with beautifully henna-ed hair that picked up the dim glow of the lone streetlight and threw rainbows of color as if a pair of prisms came up to me, and in perfect English, with almost no accent whatsoever, asked me if I were Leanne.

"Strusil asked us to pick you up. He'll pick you up in the morning at our place and take you out to his place." And that's exactly what happened.

Strusil lived way, way out in the Black Forest. It was the real Black Forest, where princesses and evil queens and magic geese came from. Strusil lived in a sweet, little ramshackle cottage behind a sweet, little ramshackle farmhouse randomly speckled upon the voluptuous snow-dappled hills with a wonderful sense of aesthetics.

There were pied cows grazing lazily against trembling greens. There was an occasional round, busty woman with round, pink cheeks in a large white apron carrying a large brown bundle hobbling up a cobbled path.

The Opposite of a Fairy Tale

Strusil and I quickly realized we didn't really like each other, but I had absolutely no money to move on. I was waiting for my final check from WomenSports. I was down to my last $20.

Strusil left early every morning to go to school and came home way after dark. He never asked me if I wanted to go into town, and I never asked if I could go. Instead, I stayed there all day in that freezing German cottage, bringing in lump after lump of coal to keep the small stove burning. I was freezing. I lay in Strusil's tiny bed most of the day to keep warm. I ate prunes and fresh yogurt, the only foods I could find. I read Alan Watts and Krishnamurti. I tried to accept. I tried not to bemoan. I tried hard not to desire.

On the third day, I took a walk down the road. I was dying for a cigarette. It was snowing. Hallelujah. There was a cigarette machine about a half a mile down the lane, in the middle of nowhere. I couldn't believe my luck, although frankly, I felt I deserved it.

There were eight brands of cigarettes I'd never seen before. One of them was "California." I bought the California cigarettes. It was such a coincidence. I really liked the irony and coincidence of finding cigarettes named after my home state in the middle of German nowhere. That was probably the best thing that happened in Germany.

The worst thing that happened in Germany was the sex between Strusil and me. It wasn't the quality of it, although that was awful. It was the mere existence of it at all. It was the wrongest sex I'd had since Baja. I mean, Strusil and I didn't like each other. I mean, I looked at his feet, his elbows, his nostrils, and I hated the look of them, the angles, the arcs. But I lay in Strusil's tiny bed all day, and then with him every night. For ten days I hammed it up just to keep myself alive, and oddly grounded. The theatrics were all I had.

Finally my check came, hallelujah, and on my last night in town, Strusil finally took me into town to have dinner with some of his friends at a brown German tavern with brown-knot paneling. They served brown food and brown beer. I was a vegetarian and a teetotaler.

Strusil and his friends kept insisting America had never produced an important writer in its laughably short-ass history. Then they all spit and gusted into German, pointing at me, shouldering each other, laughing.

Bob Dylan was playing in the background. "Highway 61 Revisited." They kept playing it over and over. They couldn't get enough of "Highway 61 Revisited."

Soon, their nonstop derogatory comments about America's brain began to annoy the hell out of me.

"You're so full of it," I finally said.

"Name one great American writer," Strusil said.

"Bob Dylan," I said.

"Well...phfftt..." they said.

Later that night back at Strusil's, while I was packing up my things to go to the Israeli kibbutz on the Mediterranean that was expecting me any day, Strusil blasted,

"You stupid American. Don't you realize what's going on in the Mideast. There's a goddamned war. Do you want to carry a gun? Because if you go to Israel now, you're gonna be carrying a gun. That's if you don't get shot first."

It took one second to change my mind. No guns. No Israel. It took another second to decide what I would do instead. I was going home, going back to America to champion American literature. I'd get a Master's, perhaps a doctorate.

I was feeling more patriotic than I had ever felt in my life. Actually, it may have been the only time in my life I ever felt patriotic.

Rape Update

Where was it? Occasionally, I wondered. What did I do with the memory of that horrible night? A few years had passed and it appeared to be hiding quietly somewhere. Where? Somewhere safe like my ass or my rooty thigh? Or did it sneak into something more tender, like my liver or my bladder? Did it look like membrane? Mucous? Tar?

Could it have melted? Could I have shat it out? Could it be gone? I barely remembered. Maybe it was gone.

My Right Earache

Hot bolts of pain that began at my jaw and raged through my head and neck like a devastating, cranial sun storm. That's how I would describe the symptoms of the massive ear infection I developed on the plane from London to Montreal. The pain was excruciating and had complete control of me.

Thea picked me up in Montreal and drove me to her parents' house on Long Island. I lay down on her bed and didn't get up for two weeks. I took two series of antibiotics and a boatload of pain pills. My head was enormous with pain, like wearing a planet. A bad, burning planet.

On New Year's Eve, heading into 1975, I arose from my sick bed and padded down the spiral staircase, dizzy and disoriented. Thea and her parents had prepared a traditional family meal—prime rib, Waldorf salad, black-eyed peas, apple pie. Through my fog of medication, I stared at the food. For once in my life, I was unable to eat. Everything hurt too much. I tried a spoonful of black-eyed peas so I'd have good luck, but they tasted like muddy bugs to me.

On January 6, 1975, I flew back to California, to my parents' house. My ear was still burbling and popping and occasionally, one of pain's long-lost cousins sprinted through my head, loud, like an asshole. I expected my eardrum to explode at any moment.

UC Berkeley, the only graduate school to which I applied in my new quest to become an expert and then to champion American literature, turned me down. I was shocked. I'd never been academically rejected before in my life. Could they possibly have been able to tell I was steering my boat on wind and whim and was currently drowning?

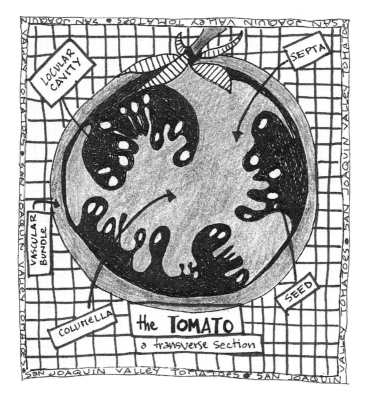

the **TOMATO**
a transverse section

SEVEN
Stockton

> *you settle upon the*
> *knobs on the*
> *dresser*
> *drawer, you*
> *decide that the*
> *secret is*
> *there*
> > —Charles Bukowski

Now What?

It took me a minute to decide that Stockton was but a quick layover to the rest of my life. There was just something about the place that irritated me. It had never fit, snug here, snug there. I got red marks from the tightness of Stockton on my

skin. Not to mention my parents, the enemy.
I couldn't stay there. I'd always wanted out.

Beginnings

"Like a little raw chicken. She looks absolutely like a little raw chicken wing."

When I was born, six weeks early, I was scrawny and pimply, with a big rash of black hair and a stunned face all scrunched up like a palsied prune.

They threw me right into an incubator to beef up, and when I reached five pounds, a few weeks later, they let me go home where people held me as if I were some kind of fish.

My grandmother Nanny held me the softest. Her skin was vast and velvety. She'd lightly smooth my hair with her curly fingers.

When I was born, it was a scorching Stockton kind of August day. One hundred and eleven degrees and still as a stone. As a kid, it was all about the pool.

Stockton was a Gold Rush town. Those were its glory days. It was a cowboy town, an aggie town, south of Sacramento 45 miles, northeast of San Francisco 90 miles. Stockton is flatter than retreat, hotter than hell, with soil richer and darker and sweeter than Denzel. Every fruit, every nut, every field crop grew to be strapping, rife.

There were tomatoes as crimson as peril. Carrots so bright, even the blind needed special glasses. Cherries that killed (in a good way) with their breathtaking baring.

There were crickets in a county-wide chorus every night giving thanks for the sleep of the hot Stockton sun after a long day of sizzling. The crickets sang. It sounded like Thank God that sun, she finally went down. Oh yeah, oh yeah.

Sometimes that sun felt like an oven, like a uranium overcoat.

Coming up in the fifties and sixties in Stockton, California, was probably almost exactly like it was in hundreds of smallish towns across America, except it was hotter, as I mentioned, and there were way more melons and bugs.

Stockton was made up of young, hopeful American families composed of wives, husbands, brothers, sisters, dogs, guppies, hula hoops, skate keys, jacks, tablecloths, lamb chops, pot roasts, noodles, potatoes, petticoats.

We had a cherry wood television console that was about the size of a garage.

I spent my time excelling in school, swimming on a swim team, riding my bike around College of the Pacific, and making cool backyard forts with Mary for protection against the spray of frustration coming in from my house.

I wore nautical, two-piece bathing suits and hid my legs with towels wrapped around my waist. I poured on baby oil and broasted in the sun between romps in the Olympic-size pool. I was always the darkest, except for Mrs. Giannini, who looked like beef jerky.

The Lilac Caddy

One good thing was my father always had an unforgettable Cadillac, and the best one was the one we had when I started driving in 1967. It was lavender. It was the color of lilacs. It was the color of your favorite Aunt Rose.

And although I had to sit on a pillow when I drove that car, which made me feel like a child, driving that Caddy was like driving a float, or a big cake.

The funniest part about the lilac Caddy was that the back seat was unhinged. So it slid around with the movement of the route like a ride at the fair. When my father was driving, and we kids were in the back, we milked it, moving into the movement, intensifying the ride. It was uproarious. We laughed uproariously.

It enflamed my father. He always started yelling at the top of his lungs. And then my mother, riding shotgun, joined in, yelling at all of us.

I took my driver's test in that lilac Caddy. Had to parallel park it. I practiced and practiced. Then failed the test anyway, but not because of parking. It was that illegal left turn they said I made.

Saved by Lonni B.

So I ran into Lonni Britton, my best friend from junior high school, on Pacific Avenue, Stockton's main old-fashioned strip, the day after I got home from Europe via Thea's. Lonni Britton. Dang. She used to be my idol, until my parents forbade my seeing her midway through seventh grade.

I think they were afraid of her. She was powerful. They thought she had too much power over me. She did. I was gaga over her imagination, her warped hilarity, her brilliance. And it did have a streak of bad. But whose doesn't?

When Lonni and I were 11 and 12 and 13, Lonni had the best brain, best jokes, best ideas, best artistic talent, best legs, best shoes, best room, and best breasts of all my friends.

I always bought the same shoes Lonni bought, but they never looked anything on me like they looked on her. They looked like plates or paddles on me, whereas on her, they looked like magical ballerina slippers. I always laughed at her jokes until I slobbered.

Lonni and I went to Macy's and filled out a bunch of applications for a teen beauty contest in the names of all the really fat girls at Daniel Webster Junior High School. It was her idea, and I knew it was mean, but I went along with it because ultimately, I was highly amused. I was giddy with amusement. A little soft-shoe with the Devil.

The contest applications were stacked in a clever cardboard display with a cutout head of a beautiful teenage blonde with perfect skin. Lonni and I filled out five applications each. I was laughing hysterically, trying to stifle it, sputtering, dribbling all over the glass countertop. Lonni was as cool as a queen.

A few weeks later, on a rare cold day, Lonni suggested we put lipstick smears on the back of everybody's thick winter coats, covertly, as they left school. I'm not sure why she thought this was a good idea, but I played along, giggling like an eight-year-old.

But by the time I got home from school that day, we were busted. My mother and father were sitting stonily on the living room couch, await, like hideous gargoyles. Apparently, Helen Leiberman had called them the minute Judy Lieberman got home from school with a big red X on her camel's hair coat in lipstick, which stains. Helene was irate, demanding not only an explanation, but also double reimbursement for the laundry bill considering all her aggravation.

"It was Lonni's idea," I said, as my father got up from the couch and began to hulk toward me.

"She's a bum!" he screamed. "I don't want that bum Lonni Britton in this house again. Do you hear me? And I don't want you in her goddamned house either. Goodbye Lonni Britton!"

My father screamed as loud as he could. It was frighteningly loud. It frightened me all those years. My eardrums vibrated and ached.

Lonni's parents showed up at our house. Her mom was prim and stout, with the pout of a faded beauty, puffy and pleated, nearly invisible. She had ice in her pale blue eyes.

"I don't want your daughter around my daughter anymore." She stared right at my father as she said this. It was probably one of the boldest moves she'd made in a long, long time.

"I don't want her over to our house, and I don't want Lonni over here either. That's it!"

Lonni's father stood in the background like an old fence post. Jack Sprat, desperately thin and gray. I imagined his legs like chopsticks. His pants hung in enormous folds. They say he drank, but I had no idea about that. All the times I spent the night at Lonni's, we stayed in the cottage behind the main house. In fact, I think I'd only seen her father twice, but that was not unusual in those days. Nobody ever saw the fathers. I think they all drank.

Lonni B., Part Three

Thirteen years had passed since I broke up with Lonni B. I think I only saw her once the whole time. She was in front of Miracle Music, Ronny Rosenkov's father's music store.

"Hey," she said. "I'm having a party at my grandmother's cabin up in Jackson. It's really great up there. You should come. There will be people you know there," she said, "like Tim Bradley and John Cooper. Steve Ring and Donny Coburn. You should come."

"Who's Donny Coburn?"

"You know. That blond friend of Michael Gold's from Lincoln. That guy with the blond ponytail."

"Maybe I will. I don't know anyone here at all."

"Well, you know me. Here. Here's an invitation. It has a map on the back. You better come."

The First Weekend of the Rest of My Life

I felt pretty the weekend of Lonni Britton's party. I liked my clothes and my body was acceptable. I had jeans I liked and a black t-shirt that had a well-designed neckline with a subliminal amount of plunge. It revealed a subliminal amount of cleavage. Nothing gaudy. I liked that.

And I made a choker the night before from a tooled gold button and a black satin ribbon. My outfit worked. It made me feel pretty. I was open to anything.

Donny Coburn started coming on to me right away. He had a sweet face, clear blue eyes, and natural white-blond hair pulled back into a natural white-blond ponytail that bolted halfway down his back like a spark of lightning. I found it phenomenal. I was really attracted to that ponytail. Goodness. It was the exact opposite of my ebony swizzle.

After whisper-talking to Donny in a corner for two hours while everyone else went to sleep, we made out on top of his sleeping bag on Lonni's grandmother's dining room floor amidst a lagoon of sleeping people. Donny and I kissed and caressed and it was pleasant, but I was desperately concerned that someone might wake up and see. I kept a slice of eye peeled at all times.

I felt massively embarrassed the next morning because of the public display. I was not a public display kind of person at all. I wore the most ridiculous expression on my face all through breakfast, like a dog that had just thrown up under the table.

I drove back to Stockton with Donny, and a few nights later, we made love in his friend's parents' guestroom about twenty blocks from my parents' house. It was the first time I'd ever had sex in Stockton. It was hard to relax. I didn't relax. I could feel my parents.

Donny, Part One

I was worried from the start that Donny might be a little slow-paced for me. If I were Hong Kong, for instance, Donny was Weed, Washington. If I were Los Angeles during rush hour, Donny was stasis. If I were *whirr*, Donny was *splat*. But after a couple of weeks, I suggested to Donny we move out of California together. I had to get out of there. I could feel them.

"Maybe Boston," I said. "I drove through Boston last year and it seemed really beautiful and alive. It's got a river running through it. Cool bridges. Or maybe Portland, Oregon. A good friend of mine from college just moved up there with her boyfriend. Maybe we should move there."

"Whatever," said Donny. "I'll go where you go."

If I was a beehive, Donny was a pebble.

Poetry, Part One

Thea moved to Portland because Frank, her boyfriend from Stanford, moved back to Portland after Stanford. I came up to visit Thea one weekend and we all went to an open-mike poetry reading at a place called The Earth Tavern. I thought it was the most magnificent night of my life. And I fell in love at first sight with open-mike poetry readings and every single poet there.

I fell in love with the poets' marvelous senses of the absurd, their silly hair and brains akimbo, ears barbed. I fell in love with their lack of convention, lack of pretension, scads of invention, silver teardrops, histrionic visions of askew. And I fell in love with the way they played their mouths and their hands like wind instruments.

I decided to move to Portland that instant, and in nine days, Donny and I were on the road for Portland, Oregon. I sold everything I could before we left, even my stereo. And the rest went into the back of Donny's ugly old Ford wagon, once white and chrome, now scabby with rust.

Taking the coast road, it seemed we drove forever. The car was slow, the road was slow, and Donny was even slower, just as I had suspected.

Luckily, the instant we entered Oregon, the landscape ruled. The sky became vast, the clouds busty and ripe with moisture. Endless hills in verdant slippers tiptoed quietly before mountains the size of planets. Trees, trees, trees, and such avuncular cliffs. It was so relaxing, like sitting on Earth's generous lap, at last.

EIGHT

Portland

And the hooded clouds,
like friars,
Tell their beads
in drops of rain.

—Henry Wadsworth Longfellow

Southeast Disgusting Street

Donny and I had one address. It was a friend of Thea's
boyfriend Frank. He said we could stay in his finished garage
until we figured things out.

We drove up to the ugliest house I'd ever seen in my life.
The house stood gracelessly in the middle of a mud-caked lot,
littered with snarls of dead shrub stems like the ghosts of an
old man's robust pubis.

It was the color of envy, the stains of the color of envy. It was a cube made out of manmade materials with a tinier cube attached. It had no porch other than four boards on cement blocks. There was not a sprout or sprig of green in the yard, just dry dirt. There was a hot breeze and the dirt was dry and floating through the air.

Four major arterials came together in a helmet of stoplights two doors down from this house. There was a gigantic, 24-hour Texaco Station, a Chevron. There were a couple of other square houses even uglier on the block, the lime of panic, the beige of ill. It was a Sunday in late August, 1975. And it was not going to do.

After two nights of sleeping on the floor of a windowless shed made out of plastic on a carpet woven from cat hair and motor oil and lint, I told Donny we were out of there or else. I was gagging.

Donny and I then moved into a tent in Frank's friend's cousin's backyard. Her husband, however, told us to leave the day after the day we set up the tent. I thought it was a personal problem. So Donny and I started looking for a house.

We found a big, old, classic Portland house, built in the first few years of the twentieth century, with gigantic rooms, no closets, no warmth, and a gasping memory of elegance creaking atop the paint-bare planes of Victorian architecture.

We moved into the house in late September with Thea and Frank as our roommates. By late October, Thea and Frank had broken up and moved out. Donny hadn't found a job, and I was down to my last couple hundred dollars.

The house was so cold, we saw our breath, and the furnace didn't work. When the furnace man came out to fix it, he told us we needed to buy oil. We'd never even heard of heating oil, being from the hot San Joaquin Valley. We also didn't have the $300 needed to fill the tank. It was mid-November.

"I thought you were going to look for a job," I whined. "I'm getting really pissed off that we're going through all my money and you're still not working."

"I know," muttered Donny.

"You haven't even looked for anything."

"I know."

"Now I'm going to have to get a job."

"I know."

Donny didn't even make up excuses. That's how slow he was.

Secretary

I got a job the next day as a part-time legal secretary downtown for a mediocre family practice lawyer who probably had Asperger's Syndrome. I was making $6 an hour and working twenty hours each week. It was a bonanza. With $120 a week, I had enough to pay my bills, and I had the time to write poetry, which was my new reason for living.

Fecal Abstracts

Donny finally got a job a few weeks later at Dammasch, the mental hospital forty miles out of town. He worked swing shift as a floor aide, which meant he did just about everything from take communion from schizophrenic Jesus impersonators, to redirect resident artists to other painting mediums besides feces.

By Christmas Eve, four months after we had arrived, we still didn't have heating oil or the money to buy it. I spent that first holiday season sitting on the couch in the middle of our gigantic living room, wrapped in a blanket I'd grown up with, eating mustard-glazed chicken and blueberry pie on a TV table. Donny had made the chicken. That's one thing. He was a good cook, and a good baker.

I watched Jackie Gleason reruns and my breath, feeling sad and cold. Yes, it was sleeting in my soul. I blamed it all on Donny, with whom, surprisingly enough, I was still having what I considered to be excellent sex.

The Abortion

in memory of poor Richard Brautigan

I got pregnant with Donny, but there was no chance in hell throughout utter infinity that I was going to have a baby with him. Not then, not later, not ever. I didn't share my feelings with Donny, nor ask his opinion. He just backed right out of the situation, quiet as a mouse, which he was.

I quashed and then blocked all sense of guilt or shame or sin or anything like that. I was merely cleaning up a mistake. That was my attitude. And my timing couldn't have been better. Scheduling an abortion was easy, especially in San Francisco. So I'd go back down and stay with friends and go to the San Francisco Women's Clinic. It was the first and most modern women's clinic in the nation. (Dare I say this?) It was almost cool to have an abortion in San Francisco there and then. A celebration of women's progress and freedom.

The women at the San Francisco Women's Clinic were perfect. They were handsome, strong, kind. They wore lavender lab wear and earth shoes. They explained everything in a clear way with a good vocabulary, kind of like 21st century waiters. But the women at the abortion clinic kept giving me time to think and feel, when I didn't want to. And they kept making me rest, when I just wanted to get on with it.

Finally they put a piece of seaweed (laminaria) up me. The seaweed was black and slimy. They said it would dilate my cervix so as to ease the retrieval of the fetal tissue. Then they told me to go walk around for two and a half hours.

"Two and a half hours?!??" Shit.

"Can I eat?"

"A small meal, like soup..."

"Let's go eat."

(Debby came with me.)

We walked a few blocks and had clam chowder in a hollowed out sourdough bread bowl on Fisherman's Wharf.

Then we got a bag of saltwater taffy. We sat on a bench. We walked around and looked at stupid key chains and kites. Finally two and a half hours passed. We went back to the clinic.

The doctor and her assistant, both honey-haired women, came out to get me. They directed me back into one of the rooms, and showed me the strange, marsupial-looking electric vacuum they would use to clean up my life. It made a high-pitched sound, a tiny screaming, like an ocelot being strangled by a lion.

I got into position. They draped me. The doctor's assistant said I'd feel a bit of cramping. I heard the mutant tapir suck and prepared for the pain. The pain was quick, not bad. The worst thing was the sound.

The women then led me into a room of cots with about six other girls on them. They told me to lie down for at least forty minutes. I lay down, but I didn't want to. I wanted to get out of there. I tried to fight the fidgeting for fifteen minutes. Then I got up and left.

Wool Walls

When I got back to Portland, Donny and I decided to move. We heard about a room in a house of Reed College students. Reed College students were known for their quirkiness, snottiness, and adventure. Whatever.

The house was wall-papered in wool, mostly plaid, as one of the Reedies was the son of a woolen mill tycoon in Vermont. The living and dining room walls were upholstered in a dark, tartan wool. The kitchen was tweed. The bathroom was pale gray flannel. I hated it. I was continually hot, itchy, and claustrophobic.

Donny, at this point, was like a boulder that had rolled to a gradual stop on a flat surface. I was like a gnat, darting for every bulb, every apple, every odor. Donny was like lava that had already cooled. I was the molten upheaval. Donny glooped like a turtle. I shimmied like an ass. There was just no subset created between us.

I grew impatient and mean. Donny stopped wanting to have sex with me. I abhorred the rejection, wept and groaned, dragging out the disintegration of our relationship as if it were a tragic opera.

Of course, it wasn't tragic at all. That was obvious to everyone but me. I mistook my abraded ego for heartbreak. I mistook truth for pain. Silly me.

I wrote about a dozen sloppy poems about Donny, but when I read them at an open mike, Virginia got up in the middle of my reading and shouted, "Bullshit. Tell the truth. This is bullshit."

"What? What'd she say?"

I pretended I couldn't really hear her, but moved out of the woolen house four days later.

NINE

The Poets

There is a pleasure
in poetic pains
Which only poets know.

—William Cowper

Love the Poets

I should have been hanging out with the poets all along. I should have been hanging out with the poets since that first night when I fell in love with all of them and their goddamned silver teardrops, instead of letting all those stupid boyfriends divert and distract me, time and time again. But, oh well.

I wrote dozens of dramatic heartbreak poems about Donny and the others, even though none of them really broke my heart, just a plate at the table of my obese ego.

I found a room to rent, got settled, and decided to go to an open-mike poetry reading again, this time at a tavern called The Long Goodbye. I was going to read my poems, cross my heart or hope to die. Thea went with me and said she would make me get up there if I tried to chicken out.

"I won't chicken out," I said.

"I know," she said.

It was a dark, smoky, multi-level bar, just as you would imagine it to be. The people, also dark, smoky, and multi-level were poured about in spills. The emcee was the same, wild-haired poet I'd fallen in love with that first night in Portland. He had a bold, vast forehead, and silly, unbuttoned jeans that kept falling down his skinny hips, barely holding on for dear life. And such terrible shoes.

I was mesmerized by this poet. I was mesmerized by how he danced to the music of his words. How he was touched by a rhythm from within, not without. And the music was hilarious and naughty and sweet and earthy. He was a tetched preacher, his voice preened and swooped, pranced and spat, comedic, insistent, entranced. He dotted every word with movement. I loved it, loved it, loved it.

"I just love him," I said to Tom, another poet.

"He's gay," Tom answered.

"Well, whatever. It doesn't matter. He doesn't seem gay," I whined.

"He's gay. There's no question about it. Gay, gay, gay."

"Well, whatever . . ."

Kurt. That was his name, the host, my poet. Kurt. He was just about to close down the open mike and I hadn't gone up to read. I couldn't do it. I was too nervous. I'd taken my poems out of the old Peechee I'd brought, but my hands were shaking violently. I couldn't do it. I put my head down in defeat. But Thea stood up and shouted,

"No, wait. My friend wants to read. She needs to read.

You need to hear her." And she turned to me and opened both arms to me, as if in presentation.

"Leanne Faye Grabel," Thea said.

"Well, come on up here, Honey," Kurt said. "Get on up here. What's your name?"

"Leanne."

"Where you from?"

"Stockton."

"No. Stockton, California??"

"Yes."

"Well, goddammit. Marjorie's from Stockton. Marjorie. Where are you goddammit? She's from Stockton. What's your name?"

"Leanne."

"Marjorie? Where are you? She's from Stockton, California, goddammit!"

Thea pushed me up on stage. The fright I was feeling could have eaten Detroit. My poems, clutched in my wet, severely shaking hands, were whipping so violently through the air that the paper was burping. I tried to hold one hand steady with the other hand as I settled at the mike, but it was useless.

Then, like magic, I opened my mouth and began to read my first poem . . .

"This is about England and France. I went there last fall." I wanted to keep my introduction short. I didn't want to bore my first audience before I even began.

London.
A muggy day.
Cold sprinkler.
Skinny hope.
Ah, to Paris.
Alan Watts doing
Neighborhood laundry.

Quick balance to comfort.
With feasting.
Pleasure, potent.
Skin, butter.

By the time I got to Cold sprinkler, I was completely calm. I was more than calm. I could feel everything I was. I was my mouth, my legs, my lips, my guts. I could feel the words going all the way through my body and out my mouth. It was kind of like singing, but not scary. And the terror slid off me, spilling down my arms, out my fingertips.

With no stories to tell.
I beg: Startle no cuddlers.
No glamour here.
Let's just kiss foreheads.
Be sofas.

The poem was done. I was calm. I read another and another. I got a big hand. Kurt came up and hugged me stiffly, ass up in the air, which is how he hugged.

"Those were very rich," he said.

I loved every second of it. I loved the other poets, so hopeful and desperate and naked and soggy. And I loved reading my poems to them. I felt like a sister, a queen, at least for a day.

"Where you from, Honey?" Kurt asked again.

"Stockton."

"What's your name?"

"Leanne."

TEN

Dickslingers

> *Never offer your heart*
> *to someone who eats hearts*
> *who finds heart meat*
> *delicious*
> *but not rare*
>
> —Alice Walker

Therapeutic Update

For the next eight years, I chose the most ridiculous, disharmonious, unavailable, impossible men possible. I chose ignorant men, macho men, redneck men, married men. I chose men who disgusted me, disturbed me. I chose men who I thought were bad. I chose men who I thought were stupid.

I guess this was a relapse. I was symbolically re-enacting.

They say victims of trauma do that, symbolically re-enact their traumas, over and over again. Perhaps that's what I was doing by falling in love with the worst, most disrespectful, manipulative, lying, horrible, scum-sucking men in the history of the world for almost a decade.

Rape Update #2

Five years had passed. I only thought about my rape when I was feeling like a failure at life. It was an easy thing to blame, a great excuse.

The memory of my rape looked like a little plastic poker chip stuck away in an old toy drawer. Or a small nodule, kind of like a wart, or a blister between my toes. Or like a hemorrhoid on my ass.

Carly Had an Idea

I was riding the ripple of the open-mike poetry scene. I went to the readings every week and was the featured poet at various readings all over town. I was feeling confident and popular. The vastly foreheaded emcee, Kurt, was now my good friend. All the male poets had at one time or another whispered sloppy, sexy things in my ear at the end of the readings, hoping to go home with me. Sometimes they did.

But then one day my friend Carly asked me if I wanted to go on a blind date with a friend of her new boyfriend.

"Don't you think Leanne should meet Thomas?" Carly said to Cliff. Cliff and Thomas had just graduated from the drug treatment facility where Carly was a drug counselor. Cliff and Carly had fallen in love.

"Great idea," Cliff said, one eyebrow up.

I admired both Carly and Cliff's aesthetics quite a bit and got excited.

Thomas and Curry and Naan

Cliff and Carly decided to have an extravagant Indian dinner in Cliff's newly rented, sixth-floor apartment with a magnificent view of the skyline, and a life-sized rosewood sculpture of Buddha that reminded me of my grandfather, for some reason. They invited Thomas and me.

I bought a new dress. I couldn't believe I found it because it was exactly what I had always envisioned. It was a summer cotton, tiny floral print, in a sophisticated pink that accepted reality. It had a halter neckline, calf-length hemline, cut on the bias, very Forties and Fifties.

And it featured me. I was dark against the pink. My hair was black and long, worn on top of my head in a high bun like a crown. Oh yes, I was ready for love.

Thomas wore a suit. It was gray and a little shiny. I hadn't seen a guy my age wear a suit since my brother's bar mitzvah. It charmed me. He was a week out of rehab and trying so hard to impress.

And a flash of light flared out of Thomas' blue eyes when I looked at him for the first time. It shot me. His eyes were the color of fresh. The blue of a spring sky. But his pupils were black and sharp like holes in that sky.

For dinner, we sat, legs crossed, on gold, silk cushions from Bali. Even the wood floor beneath us preened. Talk was easy. There were many goblets of wine and bowls of spicy, dark curries with bloated, plump raisins. And large stacks of naan, golden mittens. And then my first chocolate mousse.

"I wanted to fuck you the second I saw you," Thomas said to me later that night in the car. "I knew your pussy was going to be sweet and wet."

It was the nastiest thing anyone had ever said to me. I didn't know what to think. It was 4:30 in the morning and the dinner had just ended. Thomas was driving me home in something matronly and humble, like a white Chevy Nova.

"Do you want to come over," Thomas asked.

I nodded. I guess I did.

Thomas drove to a short, brick apartment building, opened a second floor door, pulled out a living room sleeper, put on some sheets and a threadbare chenille bedspread, and then slung his enormous penis around for the next couple hours like a lariat. I'd never met anyone so relaxed and in love with his penis. He worked it and thrust it, laughing and groaning and twirling and coddling. I just lay there making noises. I was astonished and drunk.

"It's the best thing about me," he said as I drifted off to sleep.

As a beam of full morning sun blazed through the Venetian blinds like freshly bleached teeth, somebody came into the living room from the back of the house. An older woman's voice whispered,

"Thomas . . ." And then she saw me, "Oh . . . my . . ."

Thomas jumped out of bed and shouldered her back into the hallway.

"Who was that?" I asked, horrified, when he came back.

"Nobody. Just go back to sleep."

"Was that your mother?"

"No."

"Yes, it was, wasn't it?"

"Don't worry. Go back to sleep."

"Shit." It was his mother. It was her apartment. He said it was his apartment.

"Would you like some French toast?" his mother asked, rummaging around in the tiny kitchen, which was essentially in the same room as me, abashed and entangled in her fragrant bed sheets. I couldn't even look at her.

"Sure," I peeped.

I'd been so loud. Jesus. I was so embarrassed. She must have thought I was an animal.

Ridiculous

I stayed with Thomas as monogamous girlfriend, talking about the future, for four years after that, even though just about everything he said or did made me back up or buck up or fold away. He was a political and cultural redneck who believed the stupidest things. And then he spouted off about those things loudly and crassly in front of my friends. He never made me laugh, nor laughed when I laughed, but laughed at the grossest, basest things. He made me cringe. Everyone I knew hated him. And still I stayed with him for four years and envisioned marital bliss. Jesus.

Blow Job

Once Thomas picked up a girl on the ferry to Bainbridge Island and talked her into giving him a blowjob in the men's room. We were going to visit Cliff and Carly, who'd moved up there. Thomas went to the bathroom and didn't come back until we docked, an hour later.

During dinner at Cliff and Carly's, later that night, Thomas got a phone call, right in the middle of the lamb stew. He went in another room and talked for a long time. We could hear him hooting and giggling.

When Thomas came back to the table, Cliff asked him to leave a few bucks for the call, but Thomas said it wasn't long distance. Then we all sort of realized it was someone he had just met, like on the ferry.

Later it slipped out she gave him a blowjob and of course, really liked it. She really appreciated his gigantic, ambidextrous dick. Thomas told me all about it, proudly.

Golden Delicious

Shame after shame, I stayed with Thomas. I guess I couldn't get a hold of the steering wheel. And Thomas had a plan that was very enticing since I had none. Thomas was buying a small apple orchard in Manson, Washington. He asked me to come with him. I should have taken note of the name of the place . . . well, I should have taken note of a lot of things.

> JOURNAL ENTRY:
> October 12, 1978
>
> *Apples, the apples in greenness.*
> *The apples in greenness in greenness wear droplets.*
> *The apples wear droplets like beauties wear jewels.*

Thomas and I lived in the workers' cabin on his goal orchard for the picking season that fall. We picked apples. It got old fast, especially living in the tiny, dirty cabin with Thomas and his older brother Mark.

Thomas scrambled up and down those apple trees like a squirrel, fat apples bulging from his bib sack. He'd explain the apples, shining off an area of each different apple so I could taste it. Then he would throw the barely eaten apple behind him in the trees.

The apples were delicious. The goldens, mushy in the stores, were fountains of cider in the field. Maybe this plan was going to work, as long as I wasn't doing the picking.

Running

After the harvest, Thomas went up to Alaska to crew a halibut boat, in hopes of making a big wad of money, enough for the down payment on the orchard. I was lonely when he was gone and started jogging. It felt good. I jogged everyday except Sunday. It was the most exercise I'd gotten since I was thirteen and quit activity. I was feeling great, looking great. I couldn't wait for Thomas to get back so I could show him how great I looked.

When I went to pick Thomas up at the airport one late October night, I wore really tight jeans and this fabulous pleated white blouse, a wee bit sheer, a thick red patent leather belt. People's eyes were dropping out of their sockets when they saw me, I swear. I'd never looked so good. I couldn't wait for Thomas to see me.

Thomas whooped and whistled when he saw me. Then he lifted me up. I hated that.

We went home and he immediately started slinging his lariat around. An hour later, unfulfilled on several levels, I trance-ate a three-pound bag of gorp Thomas had brought home from Alaska while he lay there, snoring, spent, prideful.

The next morning, I woke up fat.

The Final Humiliation

Thomas went up to Washington to buy his orchard. Right around Thanksgiving, he called and said he had finally arranged a deal with the owner, but he'd have to work off part of the mortgage. The orchard had a small house on it and two acres of golden delicious trees, about five years old. Thomas promised to fly to Stockton the following weekend to ask my father for my hand in marriage. That was his idea, not mine.

I flew down to Stockton. I sat in the living room with my mother, waiting for Thomas to call me from the airport. He was supposed to be arriving at any moment. Occasionally, my father lumbered out, looked at the both of us, and said something like,

"You can't squeeze blood out of a turnip." Or, "You can lead a horse to water, but you can't make it drink."

Finally, I called Thomas's place in Washington. His roommate answered and his roommate sounded strange.

"He's not home. I haven't seen him at all today."

"Where is he?" I asked.

"I don't know."

I knew that my mother knew that I knew that Thomas knew that everybody knew something fishy was going on, but my mother and I still sat there waiting for Thomas to call. I kept calling his number, over and over. Finally, Thomas called and said he wasn't coming.

"I can't get away right now," he said. "Something's come up."

Nan had come up. Nan, the born-again Christian aerobics instructor with a perfectly toned body, a stick-straight head of wheaten hair, and bad skin covered clumsily with a thick glaze of poorly matched makeup.

Thomas had actually been living with Nan and her son for months. And she really liked giving Thomas head. Again, he made sure to tell me that.

I flew to Portland the next day and then drove to Manson, Washington, the day after that. I poked around the small, shabby town until I saw Thomas's car. I think he was driving an old Chevy wagon. A '62, I think. It was parked at Nan's grandmother's house, looking utterly comfortable.

As I walked up to the door, Thomas came out and said he was sorry, but he'd fallen in love with Nan.

"Hell, she doesn't have an ounce of fat on her," he said, "except for maybe just a little sexy bit on her inner thigh," Thomas rubbed his penis through his jeans. "And she just jumps right up on it and she rides."

I was agog.

Then Nan came out, acting all remorseful, and exalted in her true love for Thomas and his true love for her. She kept saying, "It's Jesus' will."

I didn't say anything. I just shook my head in disbelief, got back in my car, and headed for Portland. I felt like a lump. A ponderous lump. A ponderous lump made out of lead. Toxic over-abundant lead.

Prunes

I felt like prunes. I stopped at a small store on the way out of town and bought a family-sized bag of prunes. They were fresh and soft. And as I drove through those dry hills away from Thomas, perhaps my worst boyfriend ever, the magnificent Columbia River Gorge twined to my left like a furrow of consideration on the brow of an angel. To my right were the contours of her belly.

I ate prune after prune. And I cried. And soon I farted and cried.

With Dan at Fran's

I drove to my good friend Fran's house. Fran hated Thomas the most of all my friends. Fran and Thomas always ended up arguing loudly whenever they saw each other. She always asked me what I was doing with Thomas, disgust dribbling down her chin.

"I don't know what you see in that fucking asshole," is what she used to always say.

Fran's friend Dan was there. Fran, Dan and I sat around her tiny red Formica table and ate prunes. And drank vodka. And ragged on Thomas. And made metaphorical jokes about prunes. I laughed so hard, I was in pain as if bursting.

So

It was now 1980, I was twenty-nine years old and I was sharing yet another drafty old Portland rental. My roommates were a male friend from Medford who was about to come out, move to New York City, become a darling in the advertising industry, catch and die of AIDS; and a pale, surly mailman, who had a giant jar of quarters in his messy room from which I pilfered one or two each day for months. He knew I was doing this, but never said a word until the day I moved out, two years later, when he handed me a bill for $53.75.

I had gone back to school for a year (who remembers?) and gotten a teaching credential. But I had just resigned from my first job teaching seventh grade English at a Catholic school (it was the only job I could get mid-year) after six weeks. I had a fatal argument with the head nun within the first month. I had assigned a writing topic asking my students to create a fantastic social order for the future. They had to imagine solutions for the problems of the world. I thought it was a great topic. but she thought it was anti-Catholic.

"God created a perfect world," she said.

Oh, for chrissakes.

Poets, Part Four

Once again, I ran back to the poets. I was making nearly full swings, here. Jumping from bad boyfriends to poetry readings to bad boyfriends to poetry readings. It was a very wide and strange arc.

There was a Tuesday night poetry open mike, now at a tavern called the Parthenon on West Burnside, a street dank and enflamed with the hiss and spank of life. Burnside divided Portland into its north and south halves. The Willamette River divided its east and west.

I had just started teaching again that week, but not in a regular school. (Screw regular.) I was teaching in a business college. My students were women who had had way too many bad boyfriends, babies, and beatings by their brutal, scarred men. And now they were trying to swim out of the rancid pudding of their lives. I was teaching them how to spell *sincerely* and *receipt*.

Their despair and determination inspired me and I had new poems about them that I wanted to read. I also had a rant about the stupid nun. And a few about Ron, a brilliant, coked-up filmmaker I'd dated for a minute until coke won. I was excited to read after so long.

Gil, Part One

I saw Gil sitting in a booth in the corner and thought Good.
A place to land. Gil.

Gil was this wild, coked-up, piano-playing Vietnam Vet
from the Bronx, hometown of my father, no less. He had that
sexy vet's jadedness. That I-just-saw-horror-and-aged-a-century-
in-a-year look that made women want to touch and provide
succor—so to speak.

Gil was chesty and wore a massive, black leather jacket and
well-worn, steel-toed boots. But he had one of those Harvey
Keitel voices, kind of high and city. He moved square, you
know, like a game piece. And he had this giant head and this
giant head of dark hair.

The night I met Gil, a few years before, he was playing
piano at a wedding. I was wearing a blatantly low-cut blouse
for the first time in my life. I had never shown major cleavage
before and was shy about it. I kept tugging at my neckline. Gil
bolted right over at his first break.

"Let it show, baby. You're looking fine." He drummed his
hips, and then mine with his squat hands, thick and veiny,
staring down my blouse. Then he began pelting me with
questions.

"So, who are you?"

"So, how come I've never met you before?"

"So, who do you know?"

"So, what do you do?"

I didn't know he was coked up because I didn't know
coke from Ajax then, but now that I think about it, I guess Gil
was coked up the entire twenty years I knew him. He learned
that in the Marines, in Da Nang.

"So, where do you live?"

"So, do you have a man?"

"So, what are you doing after the party?"

Did I answer? I don't know. Did it matter what I said?

No.

Gil sat back down at the piano and played faster and louder than I'd ever heard anyone play in my life. He was all over that keyboard, his thick, hairy hands like irritated tarantulas. I was over-wowed, but intrigued enough to stick around him.

Gil motioned me to come sit with him on the piano bench, still madly playing. I sidled up, scooted in. Then he whispered in my ear, lips touching.

"Baby, I can feel your heat."

I felt like I was seven.

Gil Part Two

Gil came home with me that night, but when we started kissing and he started clutching at me on my bed, I didn't like it at all. He was way too urgent, like he was opening and shutting drawers in search of the money or the drugs. I was cringing, crimping, suffocating.

"Wait," I said, pulling away with much muscular effort.

"What's the matter, baby?" Gil always said "baby." At first I liked it a bit, but now it was making me sick.

"Slow down. You have to slow down."

"Don't worry, baby," Gil said. "I'd never hurt you. You can trust me, baby. In fact, baby, my cock won't even get hard if you don't trust me. It can tell. Trust me, baby. We won't hurt you."

Oh, my God. What was he doing here? Why'd I invite him? What an idiot? Who was this guy? Why don't I tell him to leave? That's pretty much what I was thinking.

And then Gil started rubbing me, way too hard, too fast. As if wiping out a stain. Then I was bouncing on my bed like a toddler. I was staring at his beefy face, eyes shut tight, lips in a grimace. My head bouncing on the bed like a grapefruit.

I stared icily at Gil as he uncorked himself. He left quickly.

"I'll call you, baby," he said on the way out the door.

Jesus Fucking Christ! Did he think I was an idiot?

Nevertheless

Walking into the Parthenon that Tuesday night for the first time, alone, unknown, raw, I was glad to see Gil. He gave me an instant direction through a loud and crowded room of scary strangers. And I didn't see anyone else I knew, except a few soggy poets clustered way in the back, paddling through several puddles of discontent.

I wasn't brave enough to walk all the way back there through this crowd in front of everybody. No chance. But Gil was right there. A straight, short shot. I had to head for Gil.

Gil beckoned me to sit in his booth, but wouldn't scoot over. Instead he made room for me in the far corner. I had to crawl over him. The booth was full.

I crawled over him. He milked it. "Ooh, baby," he whispered as I slid over his lap. It was ridiculous. And after about five minutes, smashed in the corner of a booth next to Gil, I got up the nerve to enter the crowd on my own. I crawled over Gil, who again whispered, "Ooh, baby," in my ear and went back to sit with the poets. There was a lot of space back there.

ELEVEN

Sidetracked Again

> I come to wheel ruts, and water
> Limpid as the solitudes
> That flee through my fingers.
> Hollow doorsteps go from grass to grass
> ...Black stone, black stone.

> —Sylvia Plath

Desire

I finally sat down amongst my poets and began to relax, inspecting the crowd. My eyes were immediately drawn to a group of dark men with dark moustaches at one end of the long bar near the door to the kitchen. They were laughing loudly, drinking wine. And they kept bumping into each other like bear cubs, all hairy and round-bellied. They kind of made me excited.

Turns out they were Greeks. One of them was behind the bar, serving the beer. Yes. I couldn't keep my eyes off of them. I was compelled to get closer, but I was afraid to walk up to the bar.

Desire finally won out and I glided over, trying to be as small and quiet as I could be. For a split second, I looked up into the face of the man behind the bar as I ordered a Corona. A gash of light darted from his eyes, black like olives in the thick of the grove, into mine. Mystified, I twisted my head around in every direction, looking for the source of that bolt of light.

I didn't realize for weeks that I'd been seared by that one glance. I'd been branded. Who the hell was that?

"Who's that?" I asked Gil when I got back to the booth.

"Bacchus."

I couldn't keep my eyes off him. Even the tilt of his head attracted me, tilting at such a melancholy angle, as if he were remembering such an ancient pain.

And he wore a red beret. What a detail. With that black moustache. He looked like fucking Che Guevara or Fidel Castro or some other robust revolutionary.

He was, hands-down, the greatest-looking man I'd seen in years.

Kurt, the ever-present poet/host, pants akimbo, hair aloft, got up on the small Parthenon stage to start the open-mike. He screamed a skewed poem about zucchini, kind of silly, absurd, a little erotic. And then he began to introduce the twenty-two poets who were on the list, one by one. (We're talking hours.)

The poems were mostly mediocre, I thought. Wails of pity, sobs of woe. None of the poets could quite master the cheap mike, and words were either unintelligible, or too loud and distorted. Nothing worse than mediocre poetry and a bad sound system.

I was called and got up and read a new poem about one of my new students.

> These lovely brave mothers
> so young and so laden
> their futures etched in by their
> men f   a   t
> men stuffed on large failures
> their thickly-haired hands more like
> clumsy brute paws pawing
> daughters so tiny and gleaming
> their smooth skin the last ray of
> freshness and hope.

I saw Bacchus watching me from behind the bar, his head in his hands. My voice was quivering. I finished the poems and went up to the bar to order another beer. I couldn't look up in his face. Instead, I stared at his hands. They were unexpectedly beautiful. Long, thin fingers, tapered and smooth, the nails, well-shaped ovals, a slight luster to them.

He was wearing a silver wristwatch just like the one my Poppy used to wear. It had one of those stretchy bands. He kept taking it off and stretching it out, and twisting it around. He kept putting it on and taking it off. I kept staring at his beautiful hands.

Finally, I looked up at his eyes to thank him for the beer, and as he laid his black eyes on mine, like magic olives, they lured me right into their pit. And as he held my hand for a second while giving me my change, and I felt the warmth of ancient Greece, the kinship of our ancient pasts in his skin, I became lost. Went missing. It was now about Bacchus. I was totally gone on Bacchus. I was gone.

Swandiving into Hell

I started going to the Parthenon every Tuesday night for the open-mike and to see Bacchus. After a month, I got up the nerve to start talking to him. I asked him question after question: Why did you come here? When did you come here? Where did you come from?

I loved how he talked. I loved the accent, and the Greek theatre of his English vocabulary. He was always using words like soul and blood and dark.

He also called me baby, but I liked how it sounded with a Greek accent. It didn't sound as sleazy as when Gil said it.

I began staying at the Parthenon with a sprinkling of poets and Greeks well past closing every Tuesday night. I'd stay until the first twitch of dawn arrived like a chartreuse slap. I'd rush home, sleep for an hour or two, and then awake and dress awkwardly to go to my job teaching sad, beaten students how to spell separate and beautiful. I was good at my job, but I didn't look professional.

One day I was talked to about my boots. They were brown platform boots I bought at a Thrifty Drugs in Stockton. All man-made materials. I wore them with cotton mid-calf dresses, tiny floral prints.

I loved those boots. They were one the best pair of boots I ever owned. They made me taller and they made my legs look good. My legs so rarely looked good.

Satan

Then one night, three or four months later, Bacchus and I had lousy, distracted sex on the dirty, tavern floor. I knew it was coming. I could feel it coming that night. I was wearing fabulous clothes. A tango skirt the color of persimmons that had flounces, no less. A Chinese blouse the color of jade. Frog buttons. My boots.

There were no bells on a hill, no birds on a wire, no rays of light during that sloppy act of sex on that olive-oily carpeting. But there were drumbeats, some kind of deep booms. The earth moved just a little bit. Lurid spun Excitement in the air.

And there were ancient, Mesopotamian pulses.

(At least for me there were.)

The next day, walking home from work, I bonked into a four-foot granite obelisk, nose first. I was so distracted by thoughts of Bacchus, I didn't even see it. Bonk. I was stunned, literally and of course, figuratively. That bonk altered the shape of my consciousness. And re-shaped my nose.

I, yes, I know, should have heeded its import. But I didn't. I interpreted it as a good thing.

Swallowed Up Like An Ant

Sex sped things up, as always. Bacchus came over everyday. I went to the tavern everyday. Every time we had sex. Sex of some sort.

He would pick me up at lunch in his cherry red Volvo sedan and whisk me up to a bar in the hills where we'd have vodka shots with lemon twists and then make-out in his car for fifteen minutes. I would sit on his lap in front of the wheel. We'd be squished together, rubbing against each other. It was hot. I came every time.

And then he'd drop me off in front of the school and I'd walk back in in my platform boots and teach Filing and Office Procedures.

Bacchus became my food, my drink, my constant distraction. He acted like I was his. I thought I was.

Within two months, I had moved into a bleak studio apartment that smelled like hot tar and looked out on a parking lot because it was only four blocks from the Parthenon. Bacchus came over every night after locking up his tavern at three in the morning. Sometimes we'd sit in his Volvo, me on his lap, legs wrapped around. We kissed, mostly. He'd whisper sexy things in my ears about desire and wetness.

"Ooh, so wet and soft, baby." He'd say stuff like that. And our faces melded into each other. It was sizzling.

Rape Update #3

I told Bacchus I got raped in Baja and he reacted like an asshole, implying that I asked for it, implying that I liked it. Implying that we all do, we stupid women. Implying that he would be happy to act it out now if I wanted him to.

Bacchus did not supply a squirt of pathos. Not a spit. And yes, it hurt my feelings. But it didn't hurt them hard enough to make we want to walk away from Bacchus.

I wanted Bacchus. I needed Bacchus. Bacchus was the most exciting thing that had ever happened to me, except, of course, what happened in Baja. But that was then and Bacchus was now. He was sugar in my lemonade. He was catnip to my inner cat. He was guilt and fear to my religion.

Married

I knew Bacchus was married, but I
    a. blocked it out
    b. couldn't help myself
    c. didn't care

I couldn't care. I wanted Bacchus so much, nothing would get in my way. I craved him. Marriage didn't mean anything to me anyway. After growing up in such a loud and mean house, marriage didn't mean a thing to me. I didn't care if he was married. I wanted him. I was not going to let go.

And I didn't feel guilty. I felt Bacchus was supposed to be mine. He was mine. And when he left each night at four or five every morning to go home to his wife, or when I inadvertently heard somebody say something about his wife, I would cry. I would cry for hours. Sob. I'd make grief sounds I'd never made before in my life. I'd put my face in the cup of my hands. And drown in my tears. And then I'd write poems that bled all over everything.

An Ugly Part

"Why are you weeping, baby?" Bacchus asked me one night when he came over and I was weeping.

"Because Hanna saw your wife the other night and she said she was beautiful. You didn't say she was beautiful."

"It's you I love," he said. "You're my love. I love you, baby." And then he kissed me, cupped my ass. Made me wet and ready. Made me. Left.

This went on for two years. Seven hundred and thirty days. There were unintelligible phone calls from his wife. There were phone calls from his brother. There were STDs I got from him, he got from several others.

I shed galleons of tears, wrote longitudes of sodden poems, spilled the innocent juices of my heart all over the damn gravel.

Finally, after two years, I gave. I just couldn't take it anymore. I gave.

"I'm out of here, baby," I said one Wednesday morning in front of my apartment building on his lap in the car. "This feels like the Apocalypse to me." It did. I felt like I was dying of heartbreak.

"I'm sorry, baby. Don't worry, baby," is what he said. "Don't worry, baby," and then he pulled me onto his lap and lifted up my skirt.

And then he talked me back. And nothing changed. I was attached to Bacchus like a barnacle. And every night he walked away from me to go home to his wife broke my heart as if it were a pretzel crisp. My blood darkened.

Then one day, at least two years into it, Bacchus announced he would spend the night with me. Finally. He said his wife was going to Crete, and he wasn't going. He said he wanted to come over and spend the night.

I was ecstatic. I rushed out and bought new sheets, fresh flowers, French wine, a black slip, perfume.

Bacchus came over around 6:00. We kissed, drank some wine, ate, rolled on my bed, drank some ouzo. I got a stomachache, felt my skin melt into his. And then just as I was drifting off into sleep, Bacchus began fighting my bed sheets as if they were tethers.

"Jesus Christ," I said, turning over to face him.

And then he got up, got dressed, and walked out the door, anger on his face like a smear of steel.

"What are you doing?" I ran after him.

"I'm out of here," he said steely.

"Where are you going?" I felt desperate, Chinese traffic in my head. "Don't leave," I begged.

"Sorry, baby," he said.

"Why are you going?" I whined. "You said you were staying!"

"Sorry, baby, but your pillow smells."

I stared at his cold eyes.

"Your pillow smells."

I stared at his flat face. I felt like I was going to die. Right there. I lost control of my breathing. I gasped.

Okay

The next day I began packing up my life in Portland. I had to get out of there. I told people I was leaving for good. I thought I was. I'd go to Stockton first and figure it out. Where else did I have to go?

"I'm sorry, baby," Bacchus said, head down, face still flat, eyes still cold, when I told him the next morning when he showed up at around eight.

"I'm spineless," he said. "I know it. I am. But you're my love. I will love you forever."

And he grasped me and squeezed me so hard it hurt. I pulled away, "It feels like the Apocalypse to me," I said again. And it did. I thought I might die.

Bacchus came over at three the morning of the morning I was leaving forever, and he curled up next to me on the couch like my son. He wailed like some kind of sea mammal. He lay right next to me on the living room couch, and he begged me to stay. And to forgive him.

"I love you, baby. I really love you." He began to tug at me as if tugging at his mother's skirts. I didn't like it. And his fingers felt like spiders, cold and thin.

My heart's airbags had already popped open, spread themselves around me in the wreck of us. Bacchus was now buffered. I felt nothing. I wasn't crying.

"I fucking love you!" Bacchus cried.

I was stone.

At 4:30, I got in my car, my Special Edition Renault LeCar, and began driving South. Bacchus went home to his wife. I cried the entire eleven hours down, even when I stopped for a Spanish omelette in Shasta City.

TWELVE
Short Transition

> *I am the last Napoleonic soldier.*
> *It's almost two hundred years later*
> *and I am still retreating from Moscow.*
> *The road is lined with white birch trees*
> *and the mud comes up to my knees.*
> *The one-eyed woman wants to sell me a chicken,*
> *and I don't even have any clothes on.*

> —Charles Simic

Cry, Cry, Cry

I wept openly several times a day for days and days in Stockton. My mother, who hadn't wept in years, didn't say a word. Normally, she would have acted irritated by my crying, and demanded I stop. But with this sadness, she let me shed my tears.

My grandmother was dying in a crappy convalescent home called Northside Heights. My mother and I went every day to see Nanny, now 93, underinsured and overmedicated, lying in a bed all in a row, rosy-cheeked, velvet-skinned, out of her fricking mind.

We sat on the edge of Nanny's bed, petting her arms, the skin mottled and loose. We sat frozen, trying not to slip into the gully just this side of unbearable grief. At least I was.

My mother said the same things every visit.

"Mother, we're here. Mother, we're here."

"Nanny," I said, grabbing her still fleshy fingers.

"Nanny, I'm here." I barely put a toe into the vast sadness.

Then Nanny died. One day she just died. I wasn't even there. I was in San Francisco substitute teaching, going through another kind of hell. But I felt it. I called within the hour.

"She just closed her eyes," my mother said. "She looked very peaceful."

The last time I saw Nanny, a few days before, the skin on her arms felt so velvety, I thought of pussy willows. And she kept calling me Belle. That was her sister's name.

Second Funeral

The Jewish graveyard in Stockton is the oldest Jewish cemetery this side of the Rockies. But really it's this sorry-looking field in the outskirts of Stockton, where only trucks and abandoned train cars live, a few loose roosters.

When the pallbearers picked up Nanny's pewter coffin, draped in chesty pink roses just like Nanny, and the men began muttering the Kaddish, I cried so hard, no matter how hard I tried to gird my heart, its juices gushed from every pore of me.

"I'm sorry," the young rabbi whispered in my ear after the service, offering me a plastic pouch of tissues.

"Do you have a cold, or is it allergies?"

I couldn't believe what a stupid question that was.

San Francisco

I decided to move to San Francisco. I couldn't stand living with my parents another minute. They made me feel like who they thought I was before I became who *I* thought I was, and I couldn't stand their image. Or how it made me act.

I'd reconnected with some Stanford friends who now owned two apartment buildings in the Haight. Yes, it was an annoying ghost of itself, floating about in a tie-dyed sheet. But there was gentrification in the air and my friends were leading the wave.

They owned two beautiful Victorian duplexes on Cole Street, just off Haight. They'd completely renovated both of them. They lived in one and rented the other. There was a French guy named Etienne in the other. He needed a roommate. I think he was only charging me about $200 to live there.

I wandered through North Beach attempting to absorb the beloved lore of the place. I saw Lawrence Ferlinghetti and Gregory Corso one day out on the street. They were old, looked old. Corso was yelling. His jowls were pronounced. He did a horrible job hiding the shadows.

Teacher Eat Shit

I signed up with the San Francisco Public Schools to substitute teach. It started awful and remained awful. The call came in at 5:45. Then I had to figure out how to get to where I needed to get using maps and buses.

Then I had to bear the studental abuse, a behavior bred into our culture.

One morning at a high school in the Mission District, pre-gentrification, a busty, eyebrowless Hispanic girl with anarchic orange hair as large as a melon, picked up her chair and threw it at me. I was just sitting in the teacher's desk at the front of the room. It was only ten minutes into the morning. I wasn't even talking. I had just read them the teacher's instructions. They were supposed to be reading their social studies book. Then this other girl with no eyebrows jumped out the window. Then everybody laughed.

There was no way for me to know whether this girl had jumped a foot or a mile. I didn't know the building, couldn't see where she was landing. Fuck. I was overwhelmed. Tears bubbled to my eyes and began to fall just as the girl climbed back in the window. Everybody continued to laugh and look at me expectantly.

"Fuck you," I screamed. And then I walked out, shedding every stitch of teacher gear along the way. I caught a bus back to the Haight, packed up, drove to Stockton, packed the rest of my stuff, said goodbye California, and began driving back to Portland. Back to Bacchus.

Phone Call From the Monkey House

Bacchus had called the week before and wailed and barked like a seal. He had waited four months to call me. Every minute of those four months, I prayed he would call me and beg me to return to him. I expected it. I couldn't live without him and knew he couldn't live without me because that's what he said.

When he finally called, he made sounds as if he were an animal with its foot caught in the claws of a trap. He howled and whispered Baby, I miss you. Baby, I miss you.

I kept the phone to my ear without speaking.

"What are you saying?" His sounds were growing irritating.

"I fuckeen meese you, baby!" he screamed. His accent was thick. "I meese you. I fuckeen meese you."

"I'm coming back," I said.

There was a long, long, long beat of silence.

"I'll see you soon," I said.

He hung up.

Yes, I heard what he wasn't saying. But I chose not to register it. His silence literally went in one ear and out the other. I could even feel the icy whisper of air as it sped through my head.

I drove to Portland in record time, and went right over to Bacchus's new nightclub. My heart pulsed and fluttered when I saw his red Volvo parked in front. I rushed in, expecting him to be right near the door, to rush up and hug me. I expected the moment of a lifetime. But I didn't see him.

"Where's Bacchus?" I couldn't believe he wasn't there. He knew exactly when I was getting in. I called him from the road.

"I don't know," said the man behind the bar.

"His car's here. Is he in the bathroom or something?"

"No."

I looked in the bathroom. Felt frantic.

"He was supposed to meet me here. Did he say anything to you?"

"I don't know, Honey."

"Well, can you tell him Leanne's at Molly's, okay?"

"Okay."

I went to Molly's and waited. I thought Bacchus would call any minute. I waited. I waited for two days. But he never called. I tried to find him a couple more times, but he was never there.

Every bit of me ached. My appendix ached. My ganglia ached.

A few days later, I ran into a friend who told me a good friend of hers had been having an affair with Bacchus over the past two years, too. I went blind.

I wrote and mailed a note to Bacchus that night. I fretted about the line breaks and wording for three hours. I ended up with:

You're a Greek slut.
You could have been so much more.
But all you are is a
Greek slut.

That was it. That was totally it.

Like Magic

The following week, everything Bacchus had ever given me disappeared. His purple tie-dyed t-shirt, his yellow sleeveless t-shirt, the silver cigarette case, the leather jacket, the Stevie Wonder album, they all disappeared. I'm serious. Poof. They just disappeared into thin air. I thought that was rather interesting.

.

HARRY'S COFFEE GRINDER

BRAUN

WAY BEFORE ANYONE ELSE HAD ONE · WAY BEFORE ANYONE ELSE HAD ONE · WAY BEFORE ANYONE ELSE HAD ONE · WAY BEFORE ANYONE ELSE HAD ONE · WAY BEFORE ANYONE ELSE HAD ONE · WAY BEFORE ANYONE ELSE HAD ONE · WAY BE-

THIRTEEN

The Age of Harry

*I have wished to be happy
as if there were nothing else
for me to be.*

—André Gide

Harry

A few days later, I met my husband Harry. I met him the first night I slept in my new room in an old Victorian house owned by a teacher friend, far away from the Parthenon. I had a fabulous corner suite upstairs with a walk-in closet. It also had a balcony ringed with old hawthorns and oaks as if big-bellied uncles and grandpas.

My room came with a beautiful couch, the blue of summer, chubby and bright, with graceful white irises posing all over it. I sat on this couch in the middle of this room and stared out the three giant windows. The branches of the hawthorns danced against the old, wavy glass. The branches danced with the shadows. I stared. What now? What now? What now? I was kind of excited. I stuffed the sadness. I felt good.

Harry showed up that first night for a rehearsal. He was playing God in a satirical radio play written by Oregon's great literary/cultural figure C.E.S. Wood. I was invited to play an angel by one of my new roommates, who was playing Mark Twain. The rehearsal was at our house.

I had never met Harry before. As it turned out, he had heard of me, though, because he had lunch everyday at the restaurant where Thea worked. She talked about me, her friend Leanne, the poet. I hadn't heard of Harry.

Harry had a deep, booming voice, and made the perfect God. He was also hilarious, and it was supposed to be a hilarious play.

Harry walked in that night wearing a Scottish tweed cap, a thick Guatemalan sweater, and a skinny, blonde girlfriend, who appeared to be at least ten years his senior. But I could tell instantly that Harry was falling for me. He kept following me around all over the house, for one thing. And he kept talking nonstop, telling me all sorts of details about himself in a strange, random order. He had a big open face, and big open teeth like Chiclets.

First Stop, Hell

Everyone wanted to go to Bacchus's new place after the rehearsal because the main poetry open-mike was still there. I was actually supposed to be the featured act with my old percussion player Mona. The date had been set up months before, before everything between Bacchus and I disintegrated into ash.

There was no way I was going down to his new place. I didn't want to see him. I was scared to see him. But then all my new friends from the rehearsal talked me into it.

"We'll protect you," they said, acting all chivalrous.

"Come on. Let's go."

Harry didn't know anything about my long affair with Bacchus. The others knew a little, but had no idea how deeply I'd been smudged. They had no idea how heartbroken I truly was.

Drowning in Sad Rivers

I was a nervous wreck entering the bar and remained encircled within the men I was with, including Harry. It took everything I had to appear normal. I saw Bacchus stealing glances and then overtly avoiding my return glances.

Disappointment, like the smell of an old pork roast, overwhelmed me for a moment, made me reel. I was so disappointed in Bacchus. I was disappointed that he let me go, let us us go. I had loved him like water, like air, the desire so basic I mistook for breath. Heartache pulsed through me like blood clots.

All of a sudden, there in the middle of the room, I began to weep. The tears poured uncontrollably out of my face in front of everyone. It was naked, projectile weeping. It was a nightmare come to life.

I ran into the storage room behind the stage. Harry had no idea why I was crying, but he found me back there and sat by my side. I waved him out. Bacchus never even came near. I wanted him to, not Harry. I wanted Bacchus to pledge his undying love for me, but he didn't. He peeked in once, shook his head, his eyes as flat as cold cuts, dead as lamb bones.

"Can you take her home, man?" I heard Bacchus ask Harry.

"Of course," Harry said.

And Bacchus left.

Hello, Harry

A few days later, I dropped by Harry's office downtown to thank him. He worked for the City of Portland as a vocational rehabilitation counselor. I wanted to see him again and take him to lunch. I wanted to thank him for helping to sweep up my crumbles.

Harry was wearing a navy blue blazer, and a bright red tie. It was so endearing, so earnest. But he had the most horrible shoes. Crinkled up grandpa shoes.

Harry suggested a Mexican restaurant without an imagination a few blocks away. I ordered chili relleno, and Harry ordered a chicken and cheese enchilada combination plate.

Harry talked and talked and talked. He told me a lot of details about a lot of details that I didn't really find that interesting. But he held such an adoring look on his face, staring right in my eyes. He led with his teeth and his kindness. It felt good.

And yet, I couldn't follow the shape of Harry's stories. It was if his sentences were kites he had just let go of. They were already so far away, I couldn't catch them. I could barely see them. But I simply adored Harry's adoring.

First Date

Harry had a beautiful jewel of a small brown apartment. It was very den-like, very literary and male, but not manly. There was a brown couch, brown wall-to-wall carpeting, brown towels, a brown comforter, and lots of brown wood. There was also brown light since Harry's apartment abutted a larger apartment building on the east, which blocked most the natural light, turning the atmosphere brown.

Harry had grown up in a one-bedroom apartment with his mother and brother in Queens, so he was perfectly comfortable. I, on the other hand, had never lived in an apartment and found Harry's apartment to be claustrophobic. And I didn't really like brown.

"He has a goddamned coffee grinder," one of our mutual friends screamed out one night while we ate calamari and drank wine after wine. He really wanted Harry and me to get together.

"He buys fresh coffee beans, for chrissake!" he screamed at me one night. "Nobody's like Harry."

A Lapse

I ran into Bacchus on my way over to Harry's for dinner that first night. And if it were a cosmic test of my character and resolve, I failed. Bacchus looked pale and bloated. He was wearing a gigantic black leather motorcycle jacket about the size of a parking lot with about a million zippers and zipper pulls even though it was a hot day. It looked stupid. He looked greasy and ratty and fat.

"Remember when we were together, my love," he said, pulling me into his tavern and onto his lap. "Remember when you loved me," he said. He was sweating, all clammy.

He kept trying to slither his hand into my pants, and I kept pulling it out. It felt bad, like a family of snakes.

"Come on, baby," he begged. "Remember when you loved me? I still love you, baby. You're my love, my only love."

Then I let him touch me. I didn't fight him off. It seemed too silly after all we'd been through. But I didn't feel anything good. I didn't come for the first time ever with Bacchus. And when he kissed me, it felt like kissing an easy chair, like kissing hide.

I got to Harry's an hour late and mumbled something about traffic and a dental appointment. Harry accepted my excuse and just seemed thrilled to see me. He poured me a glass of Italian red wine. I think a Barbera.

He'd made a baked chicken dish—boneless, skinless breasts seared in butter and garlic, stuffed with mustard and ricotta. Each plump breast had a basil leaf on top like a pennant of renewal. Harry also steamed broccoli, mashed potatoes, made a green salad with crumbled feta on top. He'd bought gourmet chocolate ice cream for dessert.

I was very impressed. I was bobbing on the buoyancy of Harry's careful attention, feeling only a little soiled because of that dumb lapse with Bacchus.

After dinner, Harry and I walked slowly back to my house,

and made out on my chintz couch, the color of summer. One thing, however, did not lead to another. Harry wanted to wait to make a smoother transition between the old and the new. It made me feel embarrassed, for a second, but then I liked him even more.

All the Way

About two weeks later, Harry said he was ready to transition into having actual sexual intercourse with me. We lay on my chintz couch, as always. But this time, Harry slowly unclothed me. And then he relished my body with, well, relish. I felt as though I were drugged, wild, floating. I laughed, I cried. Harry stroked my face and cooed, looked stunned and happy, laughed and cried.

"I love you," he said.

Harry's Woo

Harry resigned his city job as a vocational rehabilitation counselor, and took his retirement fund in one lump sum. It was $7,400, I think. Then Harry took me out to breakfast and dinner everyday all summer long. It was fabulous. We loved and lolled and went out for coffee. We drove to rivers and beaches, went swimming, read Carver and O'Hara, Patchen and cummings out loud. We drank cocktails and nibbled more calamari. We tanned.

Sometimes we invited friends to go with us, mostly poets, as long as they had manners. Most times, we went alone.

Harry got me laughing so hard because he could mimic anyone, anything. He mimicked horses, dogs, Chinese waiters, Jewish immigrants, machinery, phones. I laughed and laughed, giddy with delight.

And for these few months, I loved touching Harry. His skin felt like cocoa in the snow, warm and sweet. Harry thought I was a dream come true—sexy, spirited, smart, cute, poetic, and sexually insatiable. He mooned over me. I gilded in it.

Oops

A few months later, I got pregnant with Harry, even though I was wearing a diaphragm and Harry was wearing a condom. It was Halloween, 1985. Harry said he knew we'd made a baby right after we did. He said he could feel it. I just remembered wild. I kind of felt like I'd been possessed like Linda Blair.

"I'm ready," he said, although he used about sixty times more words.

"That's good," I said, "because there's no way I'm having any more abortions. Bad karma."

"Then here we go," chirped Harry. "Yippee. And baby makes three."

FOURTEEN
Wifery

Either marriage is a destiny, I believe,
or there is no sense in it at all,
it's a piece of humbug.

—Max Frisch

Mrs. Harry

I had never dreamed of my wedding, which was pretty rare in the fifties, I guess, at least among the girls I knew. Most girls did. But even when I was little, I never envisioned that puffy gown of white foam, that spray of meshed tulle sprouting from my hopeful head like a fountain of pasteurized milk, that fateful unveiling, and that passionate kiss in front of everyone

I knew, including my father. No.

I didn't have any color schemes in mind. No puckered satin dresses the color of sidewalk chalk for five of my friends. No shoes dyed to match. No innumerable pearl buttons. No lemon-pepper chicken breasts. No dried out pieces of fish. No medallions of beef. No thank you notes. No. It didn't sound that appealing, didn't look that fun.

I envisioned the Olympics. The United Nations. Mansions, cathedrals. I envisioned fame, adoration, strange languages, aqua waters, not house. I played football and baseball, did challenge courses, was on swim teams. I swam the butterfly and the individual medley. I didn't play house.

But then, at age 34, pregnant again, I let my mother convince me to marry with one stare. Yes. In her one stare, I could see judgment the size of a lifetime. So I gave.

"I can go either way," Harry said, which was typical and no help at all.

"Maybe we should get married," he said.

"Oh, I don't know," I said.

"Let's do it," said Harry, hugging me as if I were his child.

Here's Harry

At six weeks pregnant, I was nauseous all the time. The only things I liked were bacon, mustard and brie cheese. Everything else tasted disgusting.

But besides the nausea, the pregnancy hormones seemed to be just what I'd been missing all these years. I felt calm and emotionally stable, perhaps even buoyant and joyful.

Plus Harry seemed to be just what my family needed, mainly because he could actually carry on a conversation with my father. The rest of us were conversationally disabled around each other. We were plugged up with the dour of Dad.

My father, chronically frustrated and irate, would choose a victim and begin to devour his victim, chewing himself into a gluttonous frenzy, spitting all over the rest of us, destroying any chance of joy or calm or cohesion.

My father's victims were us. My sister or brother were usually first. No, my mom was usually first. Then my sister and brother. I was rarely the victim until much later when I was out of his house. Until then, I was his little soldier, his one high hope.

But Harry seemed to calm him down. They drank Scotches out on the deck, and held quiet conversations, ice cubes clinking and kachinking. None of us could believe it. None of us knew how to do that, hold a quiet conversation with our father.

"It won't be easy," my father allegedly said to Harry, chuckling but serious, when Harry asked my father for my hand in marriage.

"She's very smart, you know," my father allegedly said. "But she's a moody, impatient, arrogant, undomesticated girl. It will be a bumpy road, Harry. But I like you. You have my blessing."

One Last Cup of Coffee Before I Go

I walked over the river to Bacchus's new place a couple of days later to tell him I was pregnant and probably getting married. I wanted him to stop me, fight for me.

"I want to marry you," I whined. "I do."

"We'd kill each other, baby. Don't you agree? We'd fight all the time."

See how good he was? See how he got himself out of things? Yet, he always made things seem better. It was later they seemed worse.

The Wedding

Four months pregnant and still nauseous, dressed like a fifties rocker, wearing a shiny blue suit, hair in a mullet, I wed. I was not a joyous bride. My body felt like a water balloon. My clothing wasn't breathing and neither was I.

The wedding took place in the living room of the small house Harry and I were renting in a neighborhood in which we were at least forty-five years younger and three political parties to the left of everybody else who lived there.

Harry agreed to a rabbi, and we found the most liberal rabbi we could find, which meant the least religious. Rabbi Roy. He had a ponytail, and an orange plaid shirt-tail hanging out. That shirt-tail bothered my aesthetics, but I didn't say a thing. Not to a rabbi.

My satin pantsuit was turquoise and tailored like a man's suit with a long jacket. I wore a white tuxedo blouse, a black bow tie. And as I say, a mullet, black.

I liked my outfit because the pants were elasticized, and the jacket was long and boxy, covering my belly. Harry wore vintage tails with hand-painted-by-me gold lapels.

I didn't drink, of course, but everyone else did, as expected. Everyone was gleeful, except Lola and me. She was drunk and sobbing in the restroom over her failed marriage to Michael. And I was mad because I had to stay sober at my wedding party. I was milking it a little. I'm not proud of my bridal behavior.

Meat

Meat was the only thing besides mustard and tomatoes and brie that tasted good to me. For my wedding dinner, I wanted meat, meat, meat. There was a restaurant called The Prime Rib a few blocks from our house. It was an old-fashioned steakhouse with flocked wallpaper, red on gold.

Most of my friends were vegetarians, but I hadn't eaten prime rib in years, and it sounded delicious. Prime rib was what I wanted. Prime rib and baked potato with chives and bacon bits. Salad with bleu cheese dressing. Rolls. Butter pats.

So, while almost everyone else at my wedding table chewed dried-out, previously frozen squares of halibut and squirts of creamed corn, I suckled a large slab of juicy, pink roast that looked like the tender belly of a baby. It had a nice, crisp crust, and a delicious horseradish sauce on the side. There was a fist of plump broccoli, an obese baked potato stuffed with a slab of butter, sour cream, bacon bits, chives, and a bowl of creamed spinach. There were baskets of dinner rolls wearing buttery tiaras, caped in red.

FIFTEEN

22 Years Later

> I know there are people who must be
> completely independent of others in order
> to feel free. For them, responding to someone
> else is like obeying a command. Any action
> that does not spring entirely from their
> own desires is false. I can understand this
> compulsion for detachment.

> —Jerzy Kosinski

Nocturnal Considerations

Lean forward twenty-two years, dear readers, one vertebra
at a time. It's 2002. Harry and I have been married sixteen
years. We bought a hundred-year-old house with numerous
charms and a century of dust. At my request, we painted it

pink and black. With its wrought iron fence, it looks like an illustration.

We ran a cafe for a decade for the poets. We hired a baker and three cooks. We had two dogs, although one died tragically, and one died sadly. Now, we're on our third. She looks like a lamb, and is as sweet as a lamb.

I've been a columnist and a copywriter, an editor, a poet in the schools. Harry's been this and that. We've stuffed debt in the closets like mountains of pillows and comforters.
We've grown two luscious daughters, both of them better than both of us. Both of them display our vestiges, making us beam, making us blush.

Harry and I are good friends, you can see that. We laugh and we hug and we swipe at each other. We feel happy and sad. We feel bored as a bench. We eat brie and fancy olives stuffed with garlic and feta. We drink European wine, roast organic turkeys, eat too much designer ice cream, always some kind of chocolate.

But we don't have sex. Ever. Not even on our anniversary any more. We at least used to have sex on our anniversary, but not anymore.(Making me blush.)

Sometimes, I read an erotic poem that works, full of tongues and loins, desires and odors, and my guts scream. I can only imagine how Harry feels.

I used to be the damn bombshell of the seventies and early eighties poetry scene. I had sex coming out of my ears.

Woe

So I'd wake up at three in the morning, when even the irritatingly gregarious crows are quiet for a moment, snuggling with their mommies. And I kept wondering if I was essentially dead because of what happened in Baja, not because of some sorry-ass cliché about married couples. And it began to worry me.

I tossed and turned, feverishly examining my marriage with night's superior magnification, every mote of it. Usually, around 3:45, I concluded that although my marriage resembled a fine marriage from the outside, it was actually lifeless, loveless, themeless, colorless, soggy, jagged, blazing, sharp, dull, thick, heavy, thin, different from, more arid than, less nourishing than, righter than, wronger than yours. And I was having less sex.

I panicked in the middle of the night. I scrambled to assign blame. Baja was easy, logical, there, always there.
I must need more therapy is what I thought.

Playing the Horses

I think I told you, I always choose therapists from the Women's Therapy Handbook, based on the sound of their names. It was how I used to pick the horses when my father and I went to the tracks up and down California in the late fifties and early sixties. And we used to win, based on my choices.

I looked at the names, the names of the jockeys, the colors. And then I looked carefully at the horses as they pranced by, the shape of their backs, their muscles, their sheen. I always picked the sleekest horse, the shapeliest, with the best name and the tiniest jockey.

I loved a pinto, but they were so rare. I liked a black horse, maybe, but they were usually too jumpy and snotty. A dappled gray horse always caught my eye. And a white horse was magical, but usually too skinny. With a great name, I'd pick a golden.

For a few years there, I had the touch. Greenbacks were flying through the air, baby, not ticket shreds. My father gloated and bragged, and I gloried.

So, the first three therapists I chose were named Dodie Blodgett, Harriet Hindenberg, and Miriam Golden. As it turned out, they were all amber-haired women in their forties with beautiful offices artfully furnished in minimal Nordic. They listened elegantly as I batted words about as if playing a sloppy game of badminton.

I told each of them the same story, the same way, stressed the same details, used exactly the same words and inflections each time. Oddly, from within, my voice sounded like a train. It felt like I'd lost control of its chugging along. The story was a few inches from my mouth, chugga chugga choo choo.

I Expected a Lot

I expected a lot of those first three therapists. I expected them to fix me. I expected them to lance and drain the boil of Baja once and for all. I expected them to decipher something, distill it, and feed it to me like applesauce or mashed peas. After a few bites of their pablum, I expected to turn tranquil and happy and hot for Harry.

And I expected the tight, muscular scaffolding in which I'd been encased since 1972 to relax, smooth out, turn into ramps. I expected the petrified fright injected into my bones for support in case of attack or collapse, to crumble to dust. And blow away. I expected the cure.

"So, what do you think?" I asked each therapist, my voice surprisingly sweet, always higher than I expected, a little quivery. "What should I do, do you think?"

I would have told them perhaps a three-minute version of the story of Baja.

The first three therapists said exactly the same thing, the same way,

"Well, I think you have a lot of work to do," with a long pause at the end.

"Well, I think you have a lot of work to do," with a long pause at the end.

"Well, I think you have a lot of work to do," with a long pause at the end.

"I'd be glad to see you."

"I'd be glad to see you."

"I'd be glad to see you."

I stared, sort of nodding, lightly trembling.

"I think once a week to begin with."

"I think once a week to begin with."

"I think once a week to begin with."

"Okay," I said timidly.

"Okay," I said timidly.

"Okay," I said timidly.

With each therapist, I made a new appointment for the following week. And I went the second time, still expecting epiphanies. But I left each time feeling exactly the same as when I walked in. I went a third time. Same thing. So I gave up.

I called in the middle of the night the following week and left a message saying that therapy wasn't working and I was too poor to continue and my grandmother was dying and the dog ate my homework and I quit. I sounded pathetic, self-deprecatory. I felt major relief once I made the call.

The fourth therapist gave me a tour of her newly remodeled third floor master bedroom suite upon my arrival, which made me feel sad and inadequate. Compared to her house, my house was a brochure.

The fifth was a man with a beautiful forehead and thick, snowy white hair that lifted off his forehead like an ocean wave. But at the end of the first session, he told me he didn't think I should wear red turtlenecks because they attracted too much sexual attention.

"Like now, for instance," he said, staring at my chest.

So then I tried to remember if I had put on that red turtleneck hours before with intention. No way. But it took me four sessions to get up the guts to finally quit this guy.

"Sorry, but I'm going to the coast—for eternity," I wanted to say on his message machine, but didn't. I was too chicken to be that snotty.

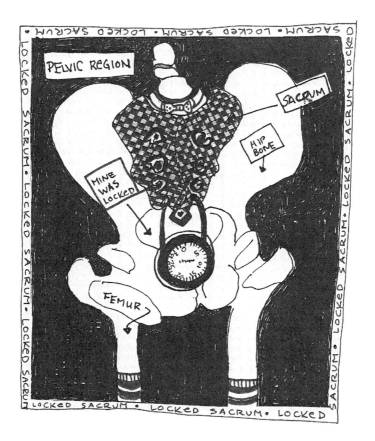

SIXTEEN

Fright Night

Only hams get cured.

—Larry, my chiropractor

Scaring Harry

One summer night in 2004, after drinking half a bottle of clear pear brandy on an empty stomach, the pear bobbing around in the bottle like a specimen, subtly thumping, after almost breaking the connubial promise hours before, but not quite, with an elfin New Yorker in a phenomenal park, I growled at Harry as if possessed by a dybbuk while sitting in the Toyota wagon in front of our house.

"Fuck me hard, Harry. Fuck me hard." I was underwater drunk, and having fun with all the histrionics. But Harry

187

didn't want to play along. He had this stiff, horrified look on his face, and he couldn't hold his erection. So he started to finger me kind of roughly. And after that, I don't remember.

The next morning, I woke up feeling alive and lighthearted, even though I had a horrible stomachache, headache, and pelvic pain. But Harry woke up with soul blight. Harry woke up with an ashen face and a coronary shiver.

"I think you need more therapy," Harry said as I drove off to buy a new cordless phone at RadioShack. My lower tract was really gurgling. I wasn't sure I was going to make it to the mall.

Later that evening, I got a hip ache. It was very insistent. It hurt to walk, it hurt to live. For the next two weeks, I went to every kind of doctor I could think of for an explanation and a cure. None of them could quite figure out what was causing the pain—not the orthopedist nor the neurologist nor the Chinese sports guru nor the acupuncturist nor the masseuse nor the magic man.

Then I went to Larry, Susan's chiropractor, and he said he thought my sacrum was locked up. "It feels like it's been locked up for years."

That night I looked up sacrum in the dictionary. The door to the pelvis is what it said. I thought that was interesting.

I called Susan.

"More body therapy is what you need!" Susan said. "Forget your mind. You need body therapy."

"Like what?"

"Like Rolfing or Reike, tapping, Alexander, or EMDR. You need to find some kind of physical inroad into the toxic clot of memory you have buried somewhere in your body. Then you can melt it down and get rid of it."

Later that week, Jana, who used to be Janet, was talking about EMDR (Eye Movement Desensitization and Reprocessing) at a Passover Seder. She said the theory was that memories could actually be reached and reshaped during a simulated REM sleep state. Eye movements could be redirected, reprogrammed, thereby changing the tone and the tenor of the memory.

This was exactly what I needed. And I liked the idea of sneaking up on my mind when it was unaware of itself and therefore unable to aggress against my better intentions.

EMDR was like taking old, crumpled memories out from their hiding places and washing them, bleaching them, ironing them, folding them, and putting them in the drawer of regular memories instead of that tiny locked chest of creepy things. Or finally tossing them out like a pair of stinky shoes.

"EMDR is supposed to be really effective for rape," Jana said.

Hmmm. It intrigued me, but I worried it wouldn't work. I'd never been hypnotized, even though I'd tried to be a few times. I just wasn't the type to trust like that, to relax like that. So I couldn't imagine how a therapist was going to put me into a REM state in broad daylight right in front of her.

But I loved the idea of rising up against my irritating mind. I wanted to revolt against its fascism. I decided to try this EMDR.

Sasha Wasserman

Sasha Wasserman, EMDR therapist, practiced in a building on the southeast side of Portland. The building was brick and cozy, with planter boxes bursting with purple peonies under every window, like children playing dress-up. The waiting room, however, was dingy, dirty looking. The curtains were water-stained. And there was an old philodendron in one corner that was so dusty, it appeared to be wearing a three-piece suit.

Sasha Wasserman turned out to be quite fat. She was so fat, her feet poured out of her shoes like a thick milkshake. I did not consider this to be a good sign at all.

She invited me into her study and asked me dozens of questions about the social and behavioral details of my life, like how I drank my coffee, how much dental work I'd had, and whether I read a book to the end if I found it boring at the beginning. Then there were a few minutes of informational blab as she prepared for my treatment, fiddling with things on her desk, back to me. I sat waiting with skepticism and delight.

"Okay," she said. "I want you to tell me about your trip to Mexico and as you tell me, I want you to follow this rod with your eyes. Keep your eyes on the lights on the rod. Just tell me the story and look at the lights on the rod. Just keep looking at the lights on the rod."

"Okay," I said.

So I told her, my voice as trainlike as it ever was. And as I chooed and chugged along, she waved that silver rod with its white lights randomly blinking in front of my eyes as if she were Leonard Bernstein. I kept waiting for my consciousness to change, but I didn't feel a thing.

When I got done with my story, which by now had been edited down to about a minute and a half, she told me to close my eyes and think of a favorite place, a pleasant place.

She told me to think of the smells, the colors, the sounds, you know, and then to imagine being there, relaxed, deeply relaxed.

Here we go, I was thinking. The audience participation part. I got nervous and went blank. I strained to envision a special place, but nothing came into my mind. Nothing. I felt pressured to choose something quickly, so I chose a generic meadow. I tried to see it—the daisies, the dandelions, the butterflies, the cool green grasses. I strained to hear it, the trickles and ruffles. I strained to smell it, its floral essences and pine.

I couldn't stop peeking at Sasha's enormous belly, which rolled over her thin alligator belt like bread dough. The woman looked like a rolled rump roast cut loose from its strings. How could I trust her?

Finally, Sasha told me to open my eyes and stare at the flare again as she waved it about in front of me. I couldn't keep my eyes off Sasha's arms, flapping like flags.

I called Sasha midweek and left a message that I had to quit seeing her because I was joining the Peace Corps and moving to Botswana.

Tapping With Zanna

Urged on by Gwennie, the funniest woman in the world, I decided to try tapping therapy next. Gwennie said it made her a different person in three sessions. She said she lost her negativity and her fear.

Now, Gwennie is melodramatic, and she exaggerates absolutely everything, so I know she didn't lose her fear or her negativity in three sessions. But she did seem different somehow, less acerbic, more relaxed.

I opened the women's therapy handbook and found her. Zanna Pax, tapping specialist. Perfect. The name had great rhythm. And great connotation (except that it sounded like an anti-anxiety medication), which, of course, was not a bad thing.

Zanna Pax turned out to be Linda Levine, ex-girlfriend of David Gold, my husband's closest friend. What a coincidence. Unfortunately, it was a bad time for David when Linda was on the scene. I remembered her dour and pale face. She was kind of creepy, really. I remembered her knotted and accusatory face. I remembered David's thin face pleated with angst.

So now she was Zanna Pax, tapping therapist. Okay. Perhaps she'd evolved, I thought. I would give her a chance. Zanna née Linda was still thin and pale and dour. Her straight brown hair was still sloppily parted, falling over and covering most of one side of her face. I did not consider that a good sign. How was a therapist going to guide me to emotional well-being with only half a face?

Zanna asked me why I was there. I told her my most recent version of the Baja story, which was down to a minute, flat.

"I see," she said, rummaging around in an antique armoire, finally pulling out an acrylic wand. She told me to follow the wand with my eyes while tapping my upper body in various places in a pattern she would lead me in until I learned it by heart. She also told me to keep talking about Baja, saying anything I wanted.

We tapped, she waved and spun the wand in her thin, pale hands. The wand was marbleized crystal, hot pink and purple, with little flecks of silver foil. My daughters used to have one just like it—when they were four—when they were dressed up as fairy godmothers for Halloween. It was hard to take Zanna seriously.

After two sessions Zanna told me she thought the rape was actually the best thing that had ever happened to me.

"It opened you up. Opened up your life."

I thought it was an interesting theory. I honestly did. I didn't take offense. I really didn't. But I quit seeing Zanna about 3:45 the next morning by phone message. That wand was just too silly for words. I think I said I was having brain surgery.

SEVENTEEN
Warped?

as for sound
I live in one great
bell of sound

—William Stafford

My Girls

Today, thirty-eight years after my trip to Baja, I find myself, as if by design, teaching language arts to incarcerated teenage girls, all raped. Their rapists were not strangers. They were their stepdads or their dads, their brothers, foster families, so-called boyfriends, as if rape were merely a part of their culture, not a trauma at all.

All of my students are in treatment for a variety of angsts, addictions, and consequent illegalities. All are wards of the state. Eighty percent of them have diagnosed mood disorders and/or learning disabilities and are receiving special education services. Their emotional upheaval, in other words, gets in the way of their success.

I feel completely comfortable amongst them, which is probably why I've kept this job longer than any other job in my life. It has been six years and I have no thoughts of moving on.

I didn't plan for this job, nor try to get this job. The job fell in my lap like one of those legendary gifts from above. One day the program chair happened to be at one of my poetry readings where I announced that I'd just rejuvenated my twenty-year-old teaching credential so I could start making an actual living. She came up to me after the reading and asked me if I wanted a long-term sub job at a treatment center school she ran.

I said, "Maybe. Let me come see."

I came, I saw, and I haven't left since. That first day, I sat in the back of a language arts classroom as beautiful girls with freckles and baby fat read emotion personification poems. Frustration was a popular topic, as was Depression.

I fell in love at first sight. They were feisty, funny, angry, sad, and hungry for love. So, here I am.

Yes, I'd say maybe ninety percent of my students are screwed for life because of rape, poverty, drugs, shitty class kismet, emotional disorders, processing disorders, social disease, physical ugliness, and, no doubt, bad food.

But I play them Miles Davis and Ornette Coleman, Bob Dylan, Joni Mitchell, the Beatles, and Glenn Gould. Most of them have never heard of Bach or Mozart. They've never heard of Jackie O, Jimi Hendrix, or the Dalai Lama. I read them William Stafford, Mary Oliver, and Charles Simic. I show them Van Gogh, Mary Cassatt, Kahlo, Warhol, and Basquiat.

Everyday I act like a clown and a fool before them. I make

them laugh, rage, and hopefully learn something, although many of them have no short-term memory so I have to teach the same thing day after day as if chiseling information into their hardened brains.

I'm the same age as their grandmas, maybe older. They've never seen anyone my age act like I do. That's good, I think. It cracks them open.

Sometimes we all cringe together. They cry, I cry. Then I make up tons of jokes about pain and sorrow, although they don't. They know that I know that they know that I know that we know, you know, though I don't tell them.

Once I told them I was raped. It was quiet for a long time after that. No one knew what to say. I don't tell them anymore. I tell you.

We listen to Louis Armstrong, but I don't tell them he smoked a joint a day for at least fifty years, although sometimes I want to.

Like A Drawer Left Out In The Rain?

So, am I ninety percent warped like they are because of what happened to me in Baja? Who the hell knows? I mean, how can I know what I would have been like if I hadn't gotten raped in Baja? What if I'd just gone skiing? Would I be better? Smoother? More hopeful? More boring? Less poetic? A lawyer? An accountant? Dead?

There's no way to know.

I don't think what happened to me in Baja was the best thing that ever happened to me, like Zanna Pax, wand therapist, said. I think it's quite a tragic story. I think I was enormously unfortunate.

Sometimes, like during the writing of this book, I cry hard for that young me. I want to squeeze her warm and hard, squeeze the freeze right out of her. The poor girl's nerves got shredded. That's what happens to The Frightened. Nerves become irradiated, permanently imprinted by the heat of the fright. Think Nagasaki.

Sometimes I look at the girls I teach and I can see their wounds deep within their eyes. I see craters and ruts filled with fire, black shadows, and glow. My wounds used to look a little like theirs, I suppose. But then I started dressing mine in rhinestones and clown noses, frockcoats and badass boots. I bought mine a birthstone ring.

I am trying to teach my girls to play with their wounds too, to dress them up in gold lamé and banana yellow cashmere, have them sit down on a whoopee cushion, or bake tiny chocolate cupcakes with tons of frosting like a pyramid rising up to the sky.

Sometimes

I look around my room, and we are all picking at ourselves, tapping our feet against the legs of our tables so fast, our shoes blur. We chew packs of gum all at once, our jaws clicking ferociously in battle with such an odd wad.

And sometimes, goddammit, we act like the warped poets life has turned us into, as if it were the only way to be.

Afterword

Everybody told me that to satisfy you, my dear readers, I must show you I learned something in the past thirty-eight years since my unfortunate trip to Baja. They said I must leave you with some kind of answer. There must be new vision. Some resolve. They said I can't leave you hungry for meaning. Can't leave you smack dab in the middle of the rainforest, without an umbrella, holding your shoes. They said I have to towel you off and put you to bed. Everybody said I have to do that.

Hmmmm, I thought. Then . . .

"Have sex with Harry," a pretty little butterfly whispered in my ear a few months ago. Where did it come from? I hadn't initiated sex with Harry in a decade at least. I hadn't had sex with Harry in two years. I confess. So I rolled over to his side, put my arms around him, and I wriggled like a snake.

Okay, it wasn't great sex, but just the existence of it at all made us both feel better. Harry felt loved, and I felt loving and hopeful and in real time. That was rare. Usually I felt loving in retrospect.

Unfortunately, right after I thought perhaps our sex life might burrow out from under us after its ridiculously long nap, Harry got a horrible sinus infection. He snored so loudly every night, I felt like I wanted to kill him. I lay in bed, kicking the mattress, Harry churning away like a boulder crusher, snorting like an orchestra of tubas.

Plus, Harry was always blowing his nose. And his handkerchiefs began to yellow up as the day went by. Harry was a veritable snot machine. It disgusted me.

All the nasal upheaval dried up my sleepy libido like a bellows working backwards. I haven't rolled over since. But Harry has sinus surgery scheduled for next week.

See, hope is still alive.

She's the one with the cookies.